ALtuitive Holdings, LLC

Growing Mentor Intelligence™
A Field Guide To Mentoring

COMPANION WORKBOOK

No part of this publication may be reproduced or transmitted in any form or by any means, mechanical or electronic, including photocopying for recording, or by any information storage and retrieval system, without express written permission from the publisher.

ISBN: 978-0-9911612-2-5

Copyright © 2014 by Alan D. Landry - All Rights Reserved.
Printed in the U.S.A.
First Print Edition

Growing Mentor Intelligence™
A Field Guide to Mentoring

COMPANION WORKBOOK

Alan D. Landry

An ALtuitive Holdings, LLC Publication
with Deuxology Publishing

Editing by Emily M. Medley

CONTENTS

Preface

Chapter 1: Fulfilling Your Greatest Need

Chapter 2: What Is Mentoring?

Chapter 3: Mentoring For Life

Chapter 4: Putting Mentorship Into Practice

**Chapter 5: The ALtuitive Method:
A Five-Step Framework for Creating Life Strategies**

Chapter 6: Tools To Empower Mentor Relationships

Chapter 7: Mentoring From The Heart

Chapter 8: Leading For Life

Chapter 9: Taking Flight

Preface

In 2013 when I began writing *Growing Mentor Intelligence™: A Field Guide for Mentoring*, I wanted it to be something mentors and mentees could use as a reference in their day-to-day activities. For the Field Guide, I compiled my own observations, experiences, and conclusions to offer an updated definition of mentoring that embraces both traditional and progressive notions about the art and science of mentoring. Going a step further, the Field Guide introduces a signature Five-Step ALtuitive Method for growing your own mentoring practice. The tools of the Method are easy to use, easy to share with others in a mentoring practice, and most importantly they are effective. I expect people will experience the Field Guide in different ways, applying the techniques and lessons to their own unique circumstances, and adapting them as they grow their own Mentor Intelligence™.

This companion workbook encourages aspiring mentors, mentees, and anyone else interested in leadership to reflect upon and document their own journeys. From my own experience, I have come to believe writing thoughts down is a powerful tool for growth and learning. If you are ready to take your Mentor Intelligence™ to the next level, then this workbook will help you do that.

The workbook mirrors the Field Guide chapter for chapter. But it also clarifies and reinforces messages and techniques – there is much new material here for you to think about and act upon. Here, you have space to start documenting your own brand of Mentor Intelligence™ and build your own mentoring practice. While you are welcome to work through the material in any sequence that works for you, I suggest you start at the beginning and work to the end since it builds from chapter to chapter. For an optimal experience, refer back to the Field Guide from time to time to see how your workbook exercises enrich the Field Guide's content.

Over time, as one's life experiences and circumstances change, these reflections can serve as a reminder that no matter who we are, where we are, or what our circumstances in life may be, we each have the power and responsibility to use our unique gifts to learn, to grow, and to apply those gifts to change our lives, the lives of others, and the world around us. I hope this workbook provides encouragement and hope as you take the time to reflect on your own mentor journey, and to share what you learn with those who are important in your life.

Chapter One: Fulfilling Your Greatest Need

In the Field Guide, the first chapter provides a foundation for understanding Mentor Intelligence™ and using it in your own life strategies and in your mentoring practice. Please take the time to center yourself on the messages in this chapter. Give yourself the gift of reflection about these potentially life-changing ideas. Then try the exercises below. The Whole Person Concept is easy enough to understand but more difficult to put into practice, especially in highly demanding and competitive environments, such as the workplace.

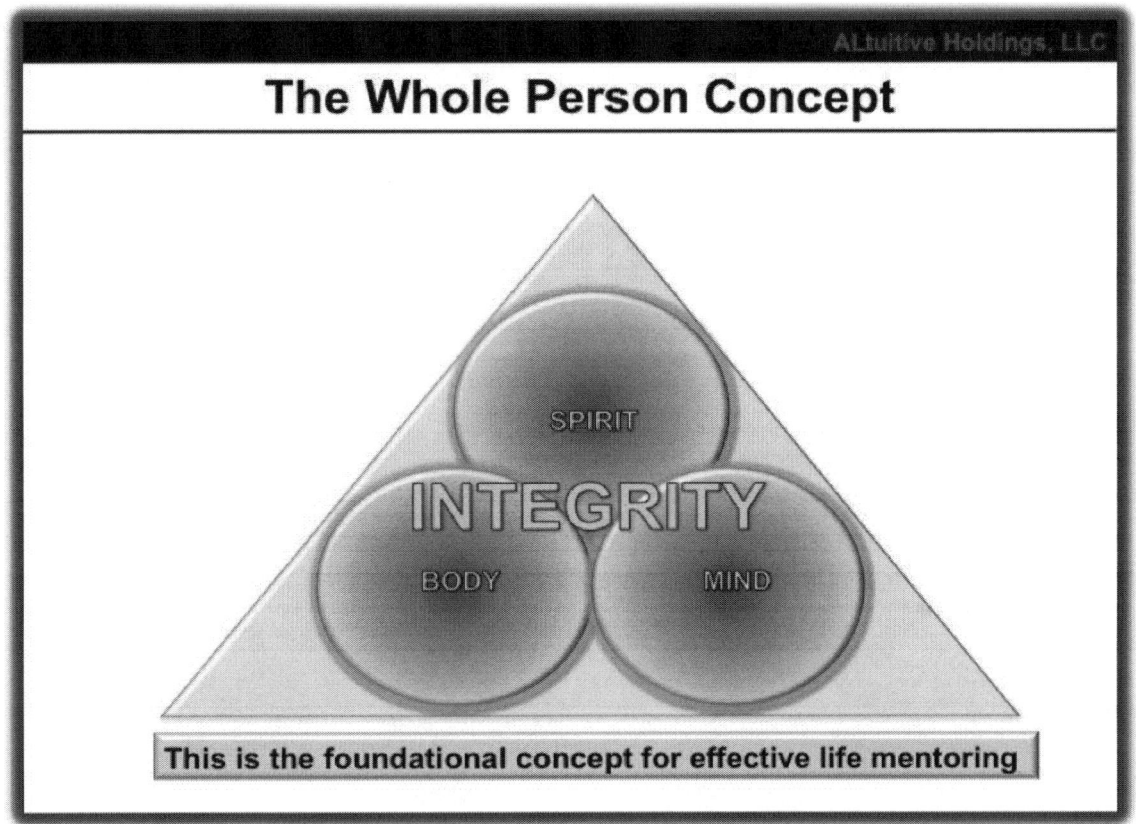

1. Whole Person Concept
Each of us brings a whole person into each relationship we develop. That whole person is a composite of mind, body and spirit. Mentor Intelligence™ is about learning how to grow in each of these components and applying that to help others grow. When we are aligned in each component, mind, body and spirit, we have integrity. When we are not aligned, we bring less than our whole self into our relationships, whether as a mentor or as a mentee.

a. What are your thoughts and observations about the notion of the Whole Person Concept: that each of us is a composite of mind, body and spirit? Is this a new concept or one you have thought about before?

b. How has The Whole Person Concept played out in your own life? In which environments has this alignment been most challenging to achieve or have certain aspects been difficult to nurture? Where or when has it been easy?

c. What does it feel like when you are misaligned in one or more area? How does that affect your relationships with others? How does it affect your work performance?

d. What do you do to nurture each area below in your own life?

Mind:

Body:

Spirit:

e. What's one thing for each area (mind, body, spirit) you can start doing today to improve your Whole Person Concept? Is it a new daily, weekly, monthly, or yearly commitment? If you put it on your schedule do you think you will be more likely to stay committed to it?

	Daily	Weekly	Monthly	Yearly
Mind				
Body				
Spirit				

2. The Workplace Connection and Integrity

The Whole Person Concept is not just about your personal life, it's about your professional life as well. Understanding this is vital to effective mentoring, both as a mentor and as a mentee. It is core to growing your own Mentor Intelligence™ and it is one of the most important things to consider when choosing who you will include in your mentoring practice.

Many people believe it is possible (and perhaps desirable) to separate who they are at work from who they are at home and in other personal settings. While that is certainly possible, the question is, "at what cost?" Sadly, in many cases I am aware of, employees do this out of fear that bringing their whole selves to work puts them at a disadvantage. But anytime a person brings less than the whole self to work, it creates a "lose-lose" situation; the workplace gets less than the person's whole potential, and the person is unable to feel accepted and complete at work. The questions below will explore the workplace connection with a goal of understanding that when we are able to align who we are at work with who we are at home, we create a "win-win" for both the business and the individual.

a. What about yourself do you feel most vulnerable about sharing at work that you share freely in your home or personal life?

b. Have you ever intentionally or unintentionally tried to separate who you are at work from who you are at home? Why did you do it?

c. How successful have you been at separating your work self from your home self? What costs have you incurred due to this approach?

d. If you bring your whole self to work and embrace the vulnerability that comes with doing this, what do you think would happen?

…worst case?

…best case?

…most likely scenario?

e. Can you identify people in your personal or professional circles who model a healthy Whole Person Concept? What have you observed about each person that makes you think this about him or her? Be as specific as you can: site habits or actions.

Name	Habits/actions of this person that model the Whole Person Concept
1.	
2.	
3.	
4.	

f. Would anyone from the list above make good candidates for mentors for you? Why or why not?

3. Building The Foundation For Growing Mentor Intelligence™
At its roots, mentoring is about helping everyone achieve potential. This requires both mentors and mentees to bring whole selves into the mentor relationship. If your mentor practice is not based on a whole person view, both for yourself and for your mentees, it could backfire and instead create confusion, distrust, and frustration on both sides. To avoid this, Mentor Intelligence™ encourages us to take a more holistic view of ourselves and each other, fully respecting differences and vulnerabilities. The Whole Person view provides a richer context for any relationship because it is based on the most personal authenticity possible – personal integrity. This is where our true human potential rests, and where real Mentor Intelligence™ is grown.

a. Are you already a mentor or have you ever had a mentor? Describe the nature of these experiences using these questions: Was your relationship in either or both cases based on a complete understanding of the whole person each of you represented? Did you feel that the relationship was authentic? Was it candid? Were the insights you gave or received as meaningful as you hoped?

b. If we accept the Whole Person Concept as the foundation for Mentor Intelligence™ what skills and disciplines do you think Mentor Intelligence™ involves?

1.

2.

3.

4.

5.

6.

7.

8.

9.

10.

Now, put a plus sign by each skill you consider to be a strength of yours. Put a minus sign by each skill you consider challenging for you. (You can use this for self-reflection and also as an interactive tool for discussing strengths and weaknesses within the mentoring relationship.)

c. When you think of the term Mentor Intelligence™ describe what that means to you at this point in your own journey, both as a mentor and as a person who has been mentored.

d. Does the term Mentor Intelligence™ help you identify ways you can grow as an individual and become better as both mentor and mentee? How does this concept add to your confidence moving forward in your mentoring practice? Does it pose certain challenges to you? If so, what are they and how can you plan to deal with them?

e. Consider applications of Mentor Intelligence™ beyond your workplace or formal mentoring practice. How could you use Mentor Intelligence™ to improve your informal relationships with friends and family? Could this bring indirect benefits to your work performance?

f. As you consider foundations for your own personal mentoring practice, both as mentor and mentee, are there any other insights you would offer that frame the foundation of what good mentorship means to you?

Notes and Reflections

Notes and Reflections

Chapter Two: What is Mentoring?

Before you enter into any mentor relationship either as a mentor or a mentee, it's a good idea to have a common notion about what to expect. To provide that common ground, we're using an updated definition of mentoring which challenges the traditional notion that mentorship is always about a wizened senior telling a less-experienced junior what he or she needs to do to be successful. In today's complex environments, traditional mentor relationships are not always the status quo and not always the most beneficial arrangements. Mentor Intelligence™ is an adapted style of mentoring that applies also to non-traditional, mutually supportive approaches where there is no senior or junior relationship involved. Mentor Intelligence™ changes the dialogue around common perceptions of mentoring by suggesting that whether the relationship is traditional or non-traditional, a questions-based approach to mentorship is most valuable and rewarding to both mentor and mentee.

1. The Basic Elements of Mentoring

The terms "mentoring" and "mentorship" are often used without agreement about what they mean. While I have not been able to find a commonly agreed-upon definition, Mentor Intelligence™ is based on **three core elements** involved in any meaningful mentor activity:

- Mentoring is a dynamic process that **takes time and energy** and evolves over time

- It is centered on creating, and investing in, **authentic relationship** between two individuals for the purpose of personal growth

- Done properly, it provides the mentee and the mentor with **access, support and knowledge** they otherwise might not get.

a. When you reflect on your previous experiences with mentoring, would you use the same words as above to describe the mentoring relationship? If so, how did the overall experience make you feel as mentor or mentee or both? If not, what words would you use to describe the relationship and how did the experience make you feel?

b. As a mentor, would you add any other core elements to your brand of mentorship? If so what would they be?

c. Have you ever *been* mentored by anyone? If you have, how would you describe the core elements your mentor based his/her mentorship on? As you build your own personal brand, what are your lessons learned and how will you apply them to your own personal style?

2. A More Inclusive Application
Not everyone is in a traditional environment of hierarchy or rank and position. What about the college student or young adult who has not yet entered the work force and desires to enter a mentor relationship with a peer? Or an employee in an organization that does not value mentorship, or include in the work culture? How can these principles and perspectives apply to family life or experiences in social clubs and other organizations? After decades of observation and learning, I have come to believe that the observations, insights and lessons learned in the pages that follow have as much application in these non-traditional mentor relationships as they do in the traditional ones.

This is a broader, more egalitarian view that puts less value on the seniority or position of a person than on the quality of the mentor relationship. Whatever your definition of mentorship, traditional or progressive, the tools, techniques and procedures of Mentor Intelligence™ have universal application and will not only improve the effectiveness of the mutual relationship, but also empower anyone who uses them to gain control over their options, their decisions and ultimately over their lives. The old adage "The more you give, the more you get" is most certainly true when it comes to mentorship, regardless of style or circumstance.

a. Have you ever been exposed to any type of peer-to-peer mentoring where there is no seniority in the relationship but still a desire to grow and learn from one another?

How was this experience different from other more traditional mentoring relationships you had experienced or were aware of?

What value did the peer-to-peer mentorship provide? What made it effective or not effective?

b. Have you ever been asked by a peer to be a mentor or asked a peer to mentor you?

How did you develop your mentor relationship? Did you meet on a routine basis? Did you use any specific approach or process in your meetings?

3. Personal "Mentoring" Styles To Avoid
Regardless of type of mentor relationship that you enter into, you should understand styles and approaches that do not work. Here are the most common failure modes to avoid. If you see them in yourself or in others, take the time to address them so the mentor relationship can grow:

- mentor who tries to "fix" something about the mentee
- mentor who has all the answers and tries to grow the mentee into his/her own image and likeness
- mentor who does not know how to actively listen or be empathetic
- mentor who does not make mentoring a priority (you can spot this style by number of cancellations)
- mentor who creates a one-way learning path (him/her to the mentee) vs. two-way
- mentor who does not invest fully or allow vulnerability in the mentoring dynamic
- mentor who stays behind his/her desk, constantly looks at watch or phone or computer during the mentoring session

a. Have you ever encountered any of these failure modes in your own mentorship journey, either as mentor or mentee? What specific failure mode(s) did you encounter? How did it make you feel? What was the overall impact on the mentor relationship?

b. If you have experienced one or more of these failure modes as a mentee, did you address it? If so, what did you do and what effect did that have on the mentor relationship? Did it make things better or worse?

c. If you have practiced one or more of these modes as a mentor, where did you learn to approach mentorship like that?

How effective was your approach? Did any of your mentees ever give you feedback about your style? Do any of them still contact you for mentorship, advice or friendship?

Would you approach it differently today?

4. Workplace/Organizational Mentor Programs
As workplaces struggle with cross-generational employees and loss of senior employees to retirement, many have created formal mentor programs to address the twin issues of knowledge transfer and employee development. Given proper resources and approaches, these programs can be invaluable to everyone involved. Unfortunately that is not always the case. Learning how to assess these programs as you encounter them is an important skill.

Pay particular attention to how mentors are assigned in your organization's program. Is the program voluntary for mentors? Is there a list of available mentors with specific skill sets? Is the program primarily focused on technical skills? Is it a quota-based program, that is, are employees required to mentor a set number of others? Is there any training available either for mentors or mentees? How many senior executives are involved? Each of these questions offers insight into the corporation's attitude and expectations about leadership and mentorship and can help you decide if the program is right for you or not. In any case, you should take the time to check it out and offer the benefits of your growing Mentor Intelligence™ to make the program even better than it already is. The exercises below will help you do this.

a. Talk to current members of the mentor program at your organization. Ask them to describe their experiences. How long have they been involved? Has the program been meaningful? What have they learned about themselves? Did the program provide increased self-awareness, access and opportunity? Are there any negative aspects about the program they can highlight for you?

Use this chart to start documenting perceptions and gather contacts within your organization who are also seeking mentoring.

Contact Name	Perceived Benefits of Mentor Program	Perceived Negative Aspects of Mentor Program

b. Contact your peers and friends in other workplaces and ask them about their mentor programs. Review the same list of questions above. Ask them to describe the most positive things about their programs, and the most negative things about their programs. Consolidate your list in the next chart and share it with your peers listed in the chart above.

This is powerful way to develop your own Mentor Intelligence™ and start having constructive discussions about how to improve mentoring practices in your workplace. These charts could also kick-start more structured discussions between your workplace and other workplaces that are trying to accomplish similar goals through their mentoring programs.

Contact Name/ Workplace	Perceived Benefits of Mentor Program	Perceived Negative Aspects of Mentor Program

5. Elite Mentorship/Leadership Programs

Many workplaces augment their basic mentorship program with much smaller leader development programs. This can be a wonderful source of learning and access for those selected. Typically such programs are extremely exclusive involving a formal selection process, special designation and status, and phenomenal access to the highest levels within the organization. If you belong to such a program, congratulations! Know that you have been tagged as someone special, and that you will most likely be placed on a fast track for advancement! Sounds great, right? It is, but I want to issue a special, personal challenge to anyone in such a program: be circumspect about your good fortune. Realize that for every one selected, there are likely hundreds of other equally qualified employees who, for lack of visibility or other circumstance, did not make the cut. Be humble in your selection, measured in your attitude, and quick to share what you can with your peers. The best leaders I have served with were humble, competent men and women, appreciative of all their blessings, and very circumspect about their gifts. A short phrase works here, and it is not a new one: "For those to whom much is given, much is expected." The day you believe that you are better than anyone else is a bad day for your leadership journey and anyone unfortunate enough to work for you.

a. Does your work organization have an elite leadership program with exclusive membership? Do you know people who belong to that program? If so, how would you describe them and how do they treat peers who are not in the program?

Would you want to work for these people? Why or why not?

b. If you belong to your organizations' elite leadership program, has this selection affected your view of yourself in relation to peers who were not selected? Be as honest as you can about this answer and consider both positive and negative responses. You might even consider asking your close friends if anything about you has changed since you were selected, and if so, was it in a good way?

c. As you reflect on your own leadership journey, what are the characteristics of the best leaders you have served with? What are the characteristics of the worst leaders you have served with?

Best Leadership Traits	Worst Leadership Traits

What kind of results did each achieve?

Best:

Worst:

How have you applied what you learned to your own leadership journey?

6. The Enabling Power of Questions

Over the years I have had my share of mentors, both good and bad. I would also suggest that at times, especially in my early years, I was probably not a very good mentor – it would take decades of exposure and experience with both the good and the bad to sharpen my own Mentor Intelligence™. Perhaps no insight over the past four decades has been more powerful or important to my mentor practice than the power of focused, intentional questions for the mentee rather than any specific answer I might try to provide.

The Field Guide explains this in great detail, but it is a key lesson, one I want to make sure gets the attention (and practice) it deserves here because it is central to growing your own Mentor Intelligence™. As you develop your own style of mentoring, focus your time and energy on learning how to ask deep questions in a non-threatening way; questions that help a mentee (and you) understand the real issues, considerations, possibilities and consequences surrounding any situation. This is a centerpiece of growing Mentor Intelligence™ and as your skill at asking constructive questions develops, so too will the effectiveness of your mentorship.

    a. Have you ever had a mentor who approached mentorship by offering you solutions he or she felt they would take if they were in a similar circumstance?

        How did that make you feel?

        Was it helpful? What did you do with that kind of advice?

b. Have you ever had a mentor who knew you so well that he or she could instinctively ask you the right questions about any situation to help you explore and understand your options rather than providing you with an answer? How did the experience make you feel about yourself and about your mentor?

What did you learn from this approach?

c. What skills do you think are necessary for a questions-based, rather than answer-driven approach to mentoring? Do you think these skills can be learned and honed over time?

d. Consider a hypothetical mentor relationship where a mentee expects a mentor to have all the answers. What kind of dynamic does this create for the mentee and the mentor?

Is there undue and unrealistic pressure in this dynamic?

If the mentee accepts the mentor's answers and fails, who lives with the consequences?

e. Consider a "questions-based" approach to mentoring as suggested by Mentor Intelligence™ and envision the dynamic between mentee and mentor. How is that different from the scenario above?

f. From both sides of the mentoring relationship, how is a "questions-based" approach potentially more effective?

Notes and Reflections

Notes and Reflections

Chapter Three: Mentoring for Life

1. Mentorship is a Basic Component of Leadership

Successful mentorship is the product of study, thought, practice and learning. It is about action, not desire. It is a discipline and as with any other discipline, it can become a way of being, a lifestyle that distinguishes the mentor. The inescapable fact is that mentorship is a basic component of good leadership. You cannot be a good leader if you are not a good mentor. This applies as much to technical fields such as science and engineering as it does to the less technical fields. Why? Because good leaders, regardless of function, must protect their organization's future by growing the next generation of leaders so the organization can be successful beyond their tenure. They invest time, talent and energy so the organization can achieve sustained growth. In so doing, they create a legacy of success that lives on in the lives of their mentees.

a. Reflect on your current ideas about leadership. Make notes below. What does it mean to be a leader? What skills and attributes do you expect for a leader to be effective? Do you believe a person can be a good leader while being a poor mentor? Have you ever worked for a person who filled a leadership position in the organization but had poor mentor skills? How did it make you (and the rest of the team) feel?

b. If you work in a technical or functional field, describe your best leader and your worst leader. Were you mentored by either or by both? What did they do differently? What did you learn to apply in your own life?

2. The Only Standard That Counts

The only standard that counts is the one you choose to enforce – the rest is just talk. If every organization were to adopt a model of mentorship where it is a basic expectation at every level, human capital would grow significantly and create a competitive advantage in the process. Why would any key leader marginalize any resource that could make the difference between survival and failure? If you want good mentorship, create it at every level, expect it at every level, and reward it at every level. It is the ultimate win-win-win solution. The organization wins with increased competitive advantage, the employee wins with life-long empowering relationships, and the mentors win with all the benefits that accrue from serving others and learning in the process.

a. Does the organization you work for require its managers (any person who is responsible for a team of one or more employees) to mentor? Is it expected at every level of the organization and across all functional areas, technical as well as non-technical? Is it rewarded? Is time allowed for it? Is there any training associated with it?

b. Are you a manager? Do you lead a team, either directly or indirectly? Do you mentor the members of your team or find other mentors for them? Does your boss mentor you or help you find other mentors? Have you asked? How important has mentoring been to your professional development and advancement? How would you describe the standard that you are setting on your team regarding mentorship?

3. The Right "Soup" and Chemistry

Good mentorship is about creating, nurturing and growing meaningful relationships. As with all relationships, this is about taking a chance on people and committing your resources to help and support them. If you have ever had a good mentor, you should be able to reflect on how the mentor committed himself/herself to you and invested in your life. The words "trust," "mutual respect" and "support" come up because there are no better words to describe what happens in an effective mentor-mentee relationship. At its very core is the care and concern of one human being for another, free of judgment and free of expectation. This is the "right soup" for a relationship that can last a lifetime!

Chemistry is an important topic to discuss, both for the mentor and the mentee. Some would argue that you should not enter or remain in a mentor relationship if the "chemistry" is not good. I am not sure that is sound advice. Chemistry can be a late bloomer. My advice is to give it time to develop. After the first three sessions, if you feel that personalities are not meshing effectively, discuss it openly and candidly and make an informed decision with your mentor partner.

Consider the times in your life when you formed an initial opinion about another person that later turned out to be completely wrong. What a shame it would be to prematurely reject what could eventually be a positive life-changing experience. Far more important ingredients in the mix are investment, candor, honesty and integrity. While chemistry has a lot to do with personality style and can unfold as the mentee and mentor both grow, investment, candor, honesty and integrity are perceptible from the outset. More importantly they are extremely hard to fake. As you enter into new mentor relationships, consider how you can create such an open and trusting relationship with a few direct questions that can set the stage from the very beginning.

a. Reflect on previous experiences you have had, both as mentor and as mentee. What is your experience with "chemistry" in the mentoring dynamic? Has lack of "chemistry" ever become a deal breaker for you in a mentoring relationship? Did the dynamics of the relationship evolve over time or were they evident from the first meeting? Have you ever been the giver or receiver of a bad first impression that changed over time? What did you learn from the experience?

b. How can you apply what you learned from your previous mentoring experiences to anticipate, mitigate, reverse, or otherwise avoid challenges arising from lack of "chemistry?"

c. How prepared are you to give chemistry a chance to develop if it is not immediately apparent?

d. How will you know if you are being effective in mentoring? What techniques can you use to discern whether you are creating the safe, nurturing environment that is the hallmark of all effective mentoring relationships?

e. Within a more traditional mentor/mentee dynamic, what can you do as a mentor to create a system of checks and balances with solid feedback loops to track your effectiveness at meeting the needs of your mentee?

4. Developing Mentor Intelligence™

Perhaps one of the most important experiential insights I have gained from my years of mentoring is the notion that there is such a thing as "Mentor Intelligence™." You may already have a sense for what this means from previous references to the term in this work and in the Field Guide. Let's take a closer look now. This is a similar notion to emotional intelligence[1] and it is a composite of inspiration, discernment, judgment, active listening, perception, empathy, and systems thinking (understanding the interconnectedness of most things in life). It is about making connections that the mentee is not able to make, and making the connections meaningful to the mentee. Primarily this is done through thought-provoking questions that point to opportunity space rather than toward any single answer.

Chapter two introduced the idea that mentorship can be built around exchanges of relevant questions from the mentor to the mentee, presented in a nonjudgmental, non-threatening way. This really is key to the magic of possibilities in mentoring. In this way, mentoring is both an art and a science. It is shaped by personal experiences, by successes, by failures, and above all, by adopting a larger systems view about possibilities, actions and consequences. It bears repeating that mentoring is not about the mentor giving the mentee answers. It is really important as a mentor that you don't appear to "have all the answers," because you don't, and more importantly, because you don't have to live with any that you offer someone else. On the mentee side, mentorship is also not about having mentors solve problems for you. Instead, both sides can use the Mentor Intelligence™ skill set to support, guide, probe, and explore – these are the tenets of good mentorship anyone can learn.

Note to Mentors: Recognize that the more significant questions become, the more difficult they may be for the mentee to answer. Honor that by acknowledging it. It is not unusual for mentees to feel lost and out of control as they struggle to understand their life circumstances or chart pathways forward. When this happens, remind mentees that no one else can make the ultimate decisions in their lives for them. They really are in control of the process. There are multiple outcomes to any situation, and that your role as mentor is to be present, to listen, reflect with them, and help them sort through choices and consequences. In subsequent chapters, you will learn a method for doing this in a non-judging but guiding way that creates trust and confidence.

Note to Mentees: As you struggle through difficult questions do not be tempted to rely on the mentor for answers to your problems. Develop your own practice of asking your mentor questions that pull out his/her expertise without demanding a perfect answer. There are no perfect answers. There are only contexts within which you can explore options and considerations. Your mentor is there to insert another perspective based on his or her experiences, not tell you what you should do.

Note to Peer Mentors: One way to approach your sessions is to take turns being in the "mentor" seat. In this way you can each have a chance to grow your mentoring skills and each have a chance to be mentored.

---

[1] Goleman, D. (1988). Working With Emotional Intelligence. New York: Bantam Books

In time, people who adopt mentorship as a way of life will increase their Mentor Intelligence™ and develop the ability to form and apply the right kind of probing questions at the right time and to the right effect. As with any discipline, the more you practice the more expertise you will gain, the more Mentor Intelligence™ you will build, and the more comfortable you will become with the art and science of mentorship.

a. Moving forward, both as mentor and mentee, what changes in mindset or practice does the concept of Mentor Intelligence™ lead you to consider for your own brand of mentoring?

b. Have you ever experienced a questions-based approach to mentorship? How was it different from your other experiences with being mentored? Have you ever had a mentor whose approach was more directive, offering answers rather than focusing on questions relevant to you and your situation? Try to describe how both approaches made you feel.

c. What kind of people do you think you will attract as you refine your brand of mentorship and leadership using Mentor Intelligence™? What qualities will you have that they will find attractive and vice versa?

Notes and Reflections

Notes and Reflections

Chapter Four: Putting Mentorship Into Practice

Productive mentoring depends on effective and receptive mentors and mentees. Mentorship involves skills on both sides, skills that can be learned and can be taught. It is also a discipline that, when practiced, can increase anyone's Mentor Intelligence™ and effectiveness as both a mentor and a mentee. In the Field Guide, both traditional mentor relationships and non-traditional mentor relationships are considered. The guidelines and practices presented there and in this workbook apply to both.

1. How to Prepare For a New Mentor Relationship
Before asking someone to serve as a mentor for you, you will need to frame your thoughts and know what outcomes you want from the relationship. Be deliberate and purposeful. Write them down and use that document to frame and set expectations once you decide whom you want to ask to become your mentor. Be honest with yourself. Reflect on the intentions and motivations that underlie your request. Make sure you are not masking hidden agendas – they will become transparent very quickly.

a. Revisit the previous questions and exercises in this workbook and gather your thoughts around the Whole Person Concept and Mentor Intelligence™. How do they fit into the context of your previous experiences, current circumstances, and future path?

You will start to see common threads emerging. These will form a useful vocabulary around what you can give and be given in a truly meaningful mentoring practice. Start a list of these key words and write them here:

b. Why do you want to enter into a mentor relationship? What are the top three outcomes that would define success for you?

        Outcome 1:

        Outcome 2:

        Outcome 3:

c. Are the outcomes above mutually beneficial to you and your counterpart? They may not be, but if there is not a direct mutual benefit, can you articulate indirect benefits for the other person that you bring to the table for them, if they invest their resources of time and energy in you?

2. Picking A Mentor and Making The Request
Following your preparation, perhaps no step is more important than selection of a mentor. Choose carefully – do some research. Does it matter to you if the mentor is in your current organizational chain? Do you want multiple mentors for the same general purpose so you can gain multiple perspectives? Where are the current pockets of mentor excellence in your organization? Leverage your social and professional networks. Ask your friends and colleagues if they know any good mentors. Approach your organizational leaders. Be visible. Let them know you are seeking a mentor and explain the kind of person you are looking for. The more precisely you are able to define what you are looking for, the easier it is for others to help you.

Once you decide whom to ask, be deliberate about <u>how</u> you ask. Make the request intentional and respectful. From my perspective, face-to-face is best, but that is not always possible. Treat the mentor with the same courtesy that you would hope to be extended to you when you are asked to be a mentor. Don't apologize for asking, and don't fail to ask because you think the mentor is too busy. All good mentors treat mentoring as a primary leader responsibility, not an additional duty to be performed when they have spare time, and they will find a way to fit anyone in who is willing to work for the support.

a. What kind of mentor are you seeking? Technical? Expertise-specific? Environment-specific? Gender-specific? Age-specific?

Is there a situation or problem driving the need that can narrow your search for the right people in your mentor mix?

b. Who is on your short list for mentors? Refer back to your list in Chapter One of role models living the Whole Person Concept. Do any of them fit into the categories you listed above? Are any of them more important than the others? If so, rank them in a list.

Name of Potential Mentor	Reasons this person is a good mentor candidate	Ranking (1= highest)

Which candidates have a reputation of making mentorship a priority in his or her schedule? Put a star by those names and you now have a really good short list.

3. Checklist For Mentees: Four Powerful Relationship Enablers

a. Be Respectful: Once you have selected a mentor, take responsibility for setting up the first session with the person who runs the mentor's calendar. Suggest a proper location for the session, one that would be comfortable to both you and mentor. Once you make the appointment, keep it. Don't be late; if a circumstance arises that conflicts with the meeting, call ahead of time. This is about mutual respect. If the mentor cancels the meeting, be understanding. If it happens repeatedly, send the mentor a note asking him/her if they are still willing to mentor you. If cancellation happens again, find a new mentor from your short list.

b. Do The Work: In your first meeting with the mentor, ask if there is a process that will be used to guide the sessions to keep you both focused and on track. If the mentor does not have one, suggest the Five-Step ALtuitive Method, as expanded upon next in this workbook and fully explained in the accompanying book, *Growing Mentor Intelligence™: A Field Guide to Mentoring* (available on Amazon.com). You could even gift copies of these to your prospective mentor as a gesture of gratitude! Because this approach is based on increasing self-awareness and discovery, there is work assigned for each session to aid that process. Between sessions, mentees to do the assigned work so there can be focused conversations that take advantage of the time available. The more prepared mentees are, the better support mentors can provide them; the same holds true for any mentor. By following a disciplined, structured process in the relationship, we always know where we are headed at any given time, how we are going to get to the next steps, and what the expectations are for each session.

c. Be Present: During your mentor sessions, dig deep, be candid, be authentic, make yourself vulnerable, and allow yourself to be uncomfortable. The more open you are to feedback, to growth and to considering new possibilities, the more effective the mentoring will be. Bring your whole self into the dialogue. Be transparent, be honest, and challenge yourself. Know that the greatest personal growth is likely found in those spaces where you are most uncomfortable or challenged. As with most meaningful things in life, the more you put into the relationship, the more you will get out of it.

d. Give It Back: The best way to show gratitude to your mentor is to learn how to become a mentor yourself. Make that part of your personal objectives, discuss it with you mentor, and keep a journal of your observations and perspectives to inform your journey over time.

4. Checklist For Mentors: Ten Critical Practices For Effective Mentoring

a. Be Gracious: Being asked to become a mentor is a special honor and should be treated as such, rather than as a burden. You may experience feelings of inadequacy or of being too pressed for time – don't give in to them. This is truly the opportunity of a lifetime and this companion workbook, along with the Field Guide, show you step by step how to guide constructive mentoring sessions—not by having all the answers, but instead by asking great questions!

b. Schedule An Exploratory Meeting: Don't wait to do this – if you do, you may forget or your mentee may believe you really do not want to be a mentor. Treat this first session as a "no-fault" meeting with either side able to opt out if things do not work out. However, be careful to avoid making a hasty decision about chemistry as previously discussed. Here is where Mentor Intelligence™ can play a major role. Many of my initial sessions over the past several years were a little rough. That is to be expected, relationships take time and energy. If you stick to it, you may find your initial impressions are wrong. If things don't sort out by the end of the third session, it's probably time to tell the mentee that you think he or she should seek another mentor, then help them make that connection.

c. Treat Mentorship As A Core Responsibility: Cancelled sessions are unavoidable from time to time, but when they become the norm, it tells a mentee about your real priorities. Leader actions will always speak louder than words. Your personal example is the best way you can establish your credentials as a mentor. If mentorship is important to you, tell your staff. I recommend that you manage mentor commitments yourself on a personal calendar rather than delegating. That way you will never lose visibility over how you are keeping your commitments to your mentees.

d. Be Present: During mentor sessions, the outside world will continue to make demands on your time. Generally, those can wait. Your mentee deserves your complete attention. Non-verbal cues such as looking at your watch, checking your phone, or looking at your computer screen indicate your real priorities – this will be crystal clear to your mentees. To avoid the temptation, simply turn off your cell phones at the beginning of the session, or leave them behind.

e. Meet Outside Your Office: Mentorship is about relationship, not about position, status or power. Your office is a symbol of your authority and it is not conducive to good mentorship. Find another place where you can meet on level ground. If that is not possible, at least move from behind your desk to establish a level playing field. While this normally applies to traditional mentor-mentee relationships, it can also apply to peer-to-peer relationships. Always seek neutral ground; that is where relationship will grow.

f. Resist The Temptation To Provide Answers: No matter how well intentioned you may be as a mentor, providing answers you do not have to live with sets the stage for dysfunctional mentoring. This critical thread was woven throughout The Field Guide because it is so important and so difficult to follow. This is especially true when a distraught mentee is asking you for your advice. Resist the temptation. Develop the situation through <u>non-judgmental, clarifying questions</u> that center around the mentee's needs and circumstances, not yours. Use questions to surface possibilities and options that they might not have thought of. Brainstorm alternatives and use your Mentor Intelligence™ to probe, guide and suggest. Offer your mentee the wisdom of your experience, and even your lessons learned, but let them come up with answers that will work best for them. By allowing the mentee to "own it" all, you set the stage for growth and learning.

g. Challenge Yourself and Your Mentees: Our deepest insecurities can provide a quick path to finding new opportunities. With sensitive, gentle, but insightful questioning based on active listening, you can make those possibilities real for your mentees. Challenge, guide and probe, but above all, support your mentee with empathy and constructive compassion. It is even more powerful when you as a mentor allow yourself to be vulnerable to your mentee. Share your failures and disappointments candidly and openly. As you do, your mentees will follow suit, and a relationship based on mutual trust and respect will result.

h. Tell your stories: While it is not helpful for you to tell the mentee what to do, it is extremely valuable for you to share your life experiences and lessons. Take risk and share your personal journey, both good and bad. Use your life experiences to illuminate ***choices and consequences***, explore them fully in the context of the mentee's current situation and focus on exploring all the possibilities. In doing so, you will broaden your mentees' perceptions and reinforce how much control they really have over any situation.

i. Be Open To Learning: Perhaps one of the most valuable and often-neglected aspects of mentoring is the process of reverse mentorship. Mentors who presume to have all the experience, knowledge and wisdom shut themselves off to the enrichment that comes from listening to, and learning from the experience, knowledge and wisdom of their mentees. This is especially true where different generations come together and perspectives on any single topic can be so diverse. If you allow yourself to learn, you can rest assured your mentees will respond in kind. Some of the most significant lessons and insights in my life have come from reverse mentoring.

j. Become An Advocate: You owe your successes to those who invested in you. Now it is your turn to share the unique resources gained from your organizational position and life experiences (your access, network, contacts, credibility, organizational knowledge, lessons learned, etc.) with your mentees. Your mentees sought you out because they believed you had something of significance to offer them. Making these gifts available to them can change their lives forever, and give your life added significance in the process. This is truly noble giving – the more you give, the more you will get in return.

Notes and Reflections

Notes and Reflections

Chapter Five: The ALtuitive Method
A Five-Step Framework for Creating Life Strategies

1. Tying The Pieces Together

Mentorship is a very personal journey. It is about creating mutual relationships and growing self-awareness. The more we know ourselves, the more effective we can be as mentors and mentees as self-knowledge forms the critical foundation for personal growth. There are many ways for a person to gain self-awareness. The ALtuitive Five-Step Method is based on integrating the discipline of strategic planning into the practice of mentorship. By taking a more intentional, deliberate approach to mentoring, with sequential steps that build on one another, we elevate the practice to a higher level, empowering mentor relationships, empowering life strategies, and increasing Mentor Intelligence™ along the way. The benefits of this strategic approach have universal application. Whether you are an individual seeking greater control over your own life, or part of a traditional or progressive mentor relationship, you can learn these techniques to create life strategies and grow as individuals and leaders.

In previous chapters, we covered the whole person foundation and we discussed the importance of focusing on questions rather answers in mentoring. The Field Guide discusses a critical insight that bears reviewing here: the swirl of questions surrounding each of us will not make sense until we make sense of the larger questions. Questions such as "Why am I here," "What are my special, unique gifts," "What does fulfillment mean to me," and "What am I supposed to give back," are all part of that set of larger life questions. It is easy to see these questions are all rooted in self-awareness, so the ALtuitive Method of mentorship begins with the quest of gaining self-knowledge. It may be tempting if you are already a successful mentor to believe that this chapter is not written with you in mind. In fact, nothing could be further from the truth. If you want to grow your own Mentor Intelligence™ to be more effective as a mentor, your journey must begin at the same place as your mentees. So my encouragement is to learn this process by applying it to your own life before you try to apply it to any other person. You may be surprised by what you learn about yourself!

2. The ALtuitive Method

There are five sequential steps in this process as shown in Figure 5.1. So who should use this process and how should it be used? While I initially developed it to support mentors interested in growing their own Mentor Intelligence™, over time it became clear to me that this process can be used by anyone who wants to grow. For those currently in good mentor relationships, it can add discipline and structure leading to more opportunities and better decisions. To those in peer mentor relationships, both parties can benefit from using it. To those who are not able to find any type of mentor relationship or who choose to not enter one, the Field Guide and this workbook can be used as a virtual mentor to provide some level of support. As with most other things in life, you will get as much out of it as you put into it.

The ALtuitive Method

Building Life Strategies Through Mentoring

- Step 1: Creating relationship and defining expectations
- Step 2: Self Awareness - creating the context for life strategies through a Personal Asset Inventory (PAI)
- Step 3: Building a Personal Development Timeline – looking forward and backward in time to frame opportunity space and to imagine desired future state(s)
- Step 4: Developing Personal Life Strategies – using a disciplined incremental approach to creating opportunity space and to achieving life goals
- Step 5: Executing the Discipline – taking deliberate actions to create accountability and move ahead one step at a time

Figure 5.1 Building Life Strategies Through Mentoring

Step One: Creating Relationship and Defining Expectations
As quickly as possible after someone asks you to be a mentor set up this first critical exploratory session. I suggest scheduling the meeting the same day that you are asked and holding the meeting within the following two weeks as a good rule of thumb. If that is not possible, contact the person who made the request and explain your timeline to remove any doubt or concern they may have.

Before the first meeting ask the mentee to provide you with the top three things he or she wants you to work with them over the next several months. If you are in a peer mentor situation you should both document what you are looking for in the relationship. Schedule the first meeting for no more than one hour. At that meeting, you should review whatever ground rules you may want to follow as mentor, mentee, or peer. This first exploratory session seeks joint commitment for the journey by openly sharing mutual expectations and understanding motivations on both sides. If you choose to follow the ALtuitive method, I recommend you use the Field Guide and this workbook to guide your sessions. If you choose a different method, make sure you both have a clear understanding of that process. At the end of the first session, decide how often you want to meet and get the meetings on the calendar.

Recently I was asked a question about whether declaring the relationship as a mentor relationship was important. It's easy to understand why this question comes up as mentor relationships frequently begin as informal acquaintances. I do think it's important to be intentional from the beginning, whether the word mentorship arises from the mentor or the mentee or the mutual partner. While it is still possible to have a mentor relationship without declaring it as such, I think it better to establish clear expectations as soon as possible, and there is no better way to do that than to ask the question directly. In any case, it is always better to create clear expectations on both sides, and declaration is the best way to make that happen.

Step Two: Building the Foundation of Self-Awareness
Personality Profile Assessment Tools
No house is stronger than the foundation upon which it is built, and so it is with every relationship in our lives. The framework of every relationship is self-awareness. Gaining authentic self-awareness is a lifetime task for each of us; there is no destination, only a journey toward discovery. How each of us perceives our personality, the impact we have on others, and how our words and actions reflect our desired self-image or contrast with it, are all food for thought and reflection.

The best mentors I know are extremely humble and reflective people, as aware of their strengths and weaknesses as they are of others'. Self-awareness is a critical component of Mentor Intelligence™. If you want to increase your Mentor Intelligence™ there is no better place to start than with your own self-awareness. This is especially critical if you are asked to be a mentor or a mentor partner. It can only help you become a better mentor and better leader yourself.

In the Field Guide there are a number of wonderful tools mentioned to aid in the process of self-discovery. If you have not done so, take the Myers-Briggs Type Indicator® (MBTI®) instrument.[2] Just do it! One of the most eye-opening initial self-awareness insights is simply knowing that there are 16 basic personality profiles and that your own profile is not better or worse than any of the other 15 profiles. It is about different preferences, not values.

Understanding how powerful our personality preferences are in creating personal brand image can be a huge step forward in self-awareness and an incredible leadership tool for teams and individuals. Books such as ***Type Talk At Work*** by Otto Kroeger, Janet Thuesen and Hile Rutledge, and ***Please Understand Me*** by David Keirsey and Marilyn Bates are wonderful introductions to the topic. The insights they provide are as valuable on the home front as they are at work.

There are many other useful instruments to include the Kirton Adaption-Innovation (KAI) Inventory[3] and literally dozens of leader style inventories available on the web. After years of working on teams and with highly educated adults, it still surprises me that so many have never even heard of any of these basic personality tools, much less used one. You cannot begin to effectively lead or mentor others until you have learned how to lead yourself!

---

[3]See Kirton Adaption-Innovation Inventory web site: www.kaicentre.com.

a. Have you ever taken the Myers-Briggs Type Indicator instrument? What is your personality profile?

What were your immediate thoughts when you discovered your type indicator? Are you an extrovert or an introvert?

How does this aspect of your style impact the other styles? How about the other aspects of your profile?

What are the personal preferences of your profile that you need to be sensitive to based on how they can hurt others?

b. Do you belong to or lead a team of co-workers? Have they all taken the MBTI? (If not, why not?)

What are the type indicators of the other members and how do the profiles drive team behavior?

How can you use this information to become a more effective team? What have you done to encourage the other members of your team to grow in their self-awareness?

c. Do you belong to any group or team that is in conflict? What is the root cause of that conflict?

Would increased self-awareness lead to better communications and conflict resolution?

What are some creative ways to lead your team through this process of enhanced self-awareness?

d. What other tools or instruments have you taken to provide better self-awareness? What important insights about yourself did you gain from each of them individually and collectively?

How can you apply that learning to your life and to your mentor practice?

Personal Asset Inventory (PAI) – A Personal SWOT Analysis
Do you want more control over your life? More structure and rigor in decision-making? Are you tired of making the same mistakes over and over again? Are you looking for a more effective tool to help you help others in your mentor practice? Are you seeking a more solid foundation for making important life decisions? Whether mentor, mentee or peer partner, a personal Strengths, Weaknesses, Opportunities, and Threats (SWOT) analysis may be just what you need. In the strategic planning process, a SWOT analysis provides the critical foundation from which to build effective strategies. It is a powerful tool that provides the basic context for strategic decision-making; without it, any strategy would rest on a bed of sand.

Since the work we are about is building <u>life</u> strategies, I created an instrument that can be uniquely applied to anyone's life to develop that context in a personal sense. The tool is called a Personal Asset Inventory (PAI), which is an amplification of the simple strengths/weaknesses analysis which most of you have probably been exposed to at some point in your life. Through this tool we can create a "living" personal SWOT - a snapshot in time that documents the things that are important to you and defines the unique context that should underlie every one of your important life decisions.

This tool can be used in a number of ways. If you are a mentor, you can use this tool to help your mentees create a baseline for their life strategies. If you are a mentee, you can use this tool to provide deeper insights that can be used to aid your decision-making in the context of the unique person that you are. Then as your life circumstances change, you can revise your PAI to provide a new baseline for your decision-making. If you are in a peer mentor relationship, you can both take advantage of the special insights such a tool can provide. Regardless of situation, a tangible life strategy begins here.

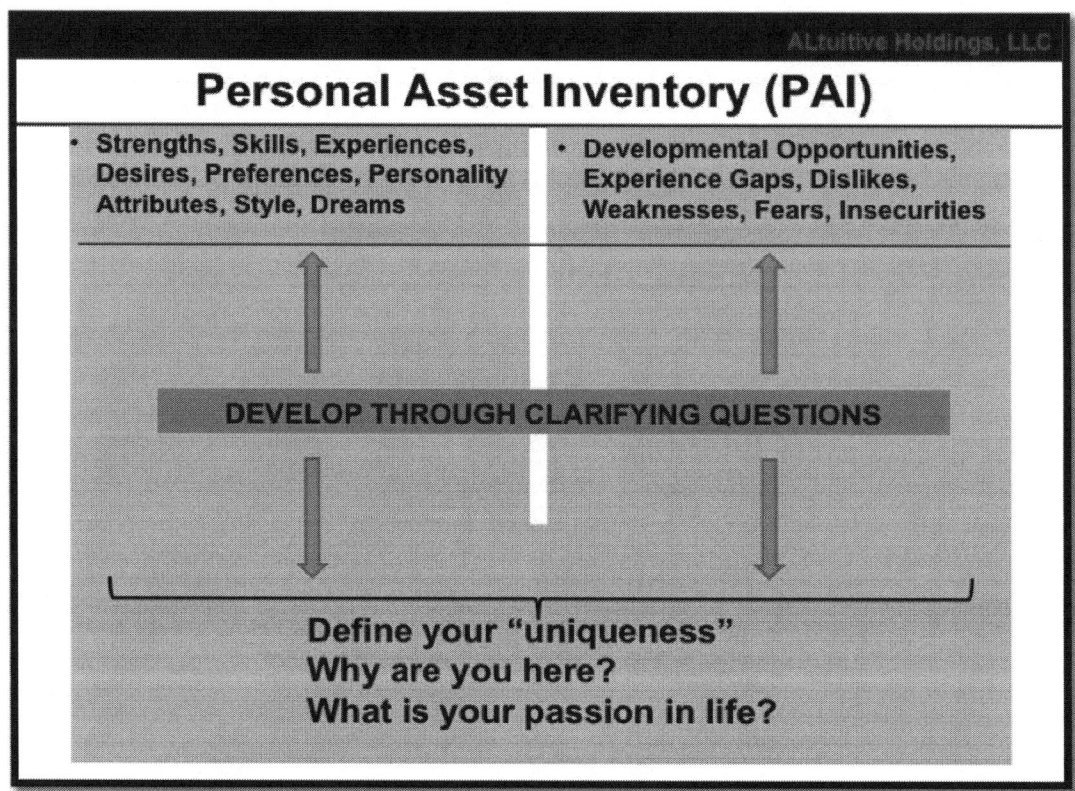

Figure 5.2 Personal Asset Inventory (PAI)

The tool is very simple to use. All it takes is a single sheet of paper, a ruler to draw a couple of lines, and candor. As Figure 5.2 illustrates, on the left side of the paper record your strengths, skills, experiences, desires, preferences, styles, likes and dreams. I recommend creating a list of single words or simple phrases that capture the central idea rather than sentences.

Don't worry about priorities yet, the idea is to brainstorm the things most critical to you and get them down quickly. On the right side of the paper, list weaknesses, developmental opportunities, experience gaps, dislikes, fears and insecurities. Again, the idea is to put down in writing the things most important to you – these are the critical items that you would want to consider in making any important decision.

In my mentor practice, the mentee builds this chart as homework to be completed between the first and the second session. We use the completed chart as a guide to explore answers to the three questions at the bottom of the chart. By augmenting the knowledge gained from this tool with other instruments and properly focused questions, I have been able to help my mentees define their uniqueness and better understand their personal passions in life and the values that underline them.

I believe that people are happiest when they are able to align their work life with their personal life. The process of revealing each mentee's specialness in these broader categories builds a solid foundation from which to evaluate any critical life decision and create meaningful life strategies. This is the base piece on which everything else depends, so we take the time to work it carefully and intentionally.

a. Suggested Activity: Create your own Personal Asset Inventory by populating the fields below. For simplicity I have just listed strengths and weaknesses; however, be sure to include the expanded attributes detailed above.

STRENGTHS	WEAKNESSES

b. Suggested Follow-on Activity: We all have "blind spots" in self-awareness, differences between how we perceive ourselves and how others in fact perceive us. These "blind spots" are an important part of self-awareness. To identify them, you can use this simple activity. Give a blank 3x5 card to ten different people who know you. Try to make the group as diverse as possible including family, friends and co-workers. Ask each person to list three words/short phrases that best describe you. Collect the cards and write their input below.

c. Based on test instruments, your Personal Asset Inventory, and the insights gained from your 3x5 cards, do your best to answer the following questions:

(1) What are the characteristics that best define your uniqueness?

(2) Why do you think that you are here on this Earth? What is the purpose of your life?

(3) What are your talents? What are you most passionate about?

At the end of these exercises, you will have a more informed understanding of who you are, how others perceive you, and what your unique talents are. If you serve as a mentor to others and guide them through this process, your relationship will grow and you will be better able to help them align decisions with their passions, skills and attributes, personal goals and aspirations, and unique gifts. These frame the larger questions of life for each of us, and they deserve our time, attention and focus as mentors, mentees and partners. I encourage you to bring the PAI into each of your mentor sessions. Talk about the results. Listen carefully and intently – this is active listening. Be encouraging and supportive yet deliberate and discerning as you grow to understand your mentees more fully and you help them understand themselves. Ask non-judgmental, clarifying questions. Help mentees understand their potential and possibilities for the future with a clear understanding of consequences for each path considered.

Step 3: Building A Personal Development Timeline

The next step in the ALtuitive Method is to create a Personal Development Timeline. As with the other tools in this process, the Personal Development Timeline has as much meaning for an individual who does not have a mentor and wants to grow as it does for the mentor who is helping his/her mentees create life strategies.

The notion is a simple one – lay out your life from the time you graduated from school and entered the workforce until a date 25-30 years in the future noting critical decision points, your personal vision and the skills, knowledge, attributes and experiences it would take you to make that vision real! Sounds pretty simple doesn't it? In reality, most people have a hard time identifying what/who/where they want to be that far in the future.

Figure 5.3 shows a notional Personal Development Timeline with central elements. After you spend a little time thinking about what this entails, reflect on what your Personal Development Timeline would look like. Perfect! Now it's time to make your own!

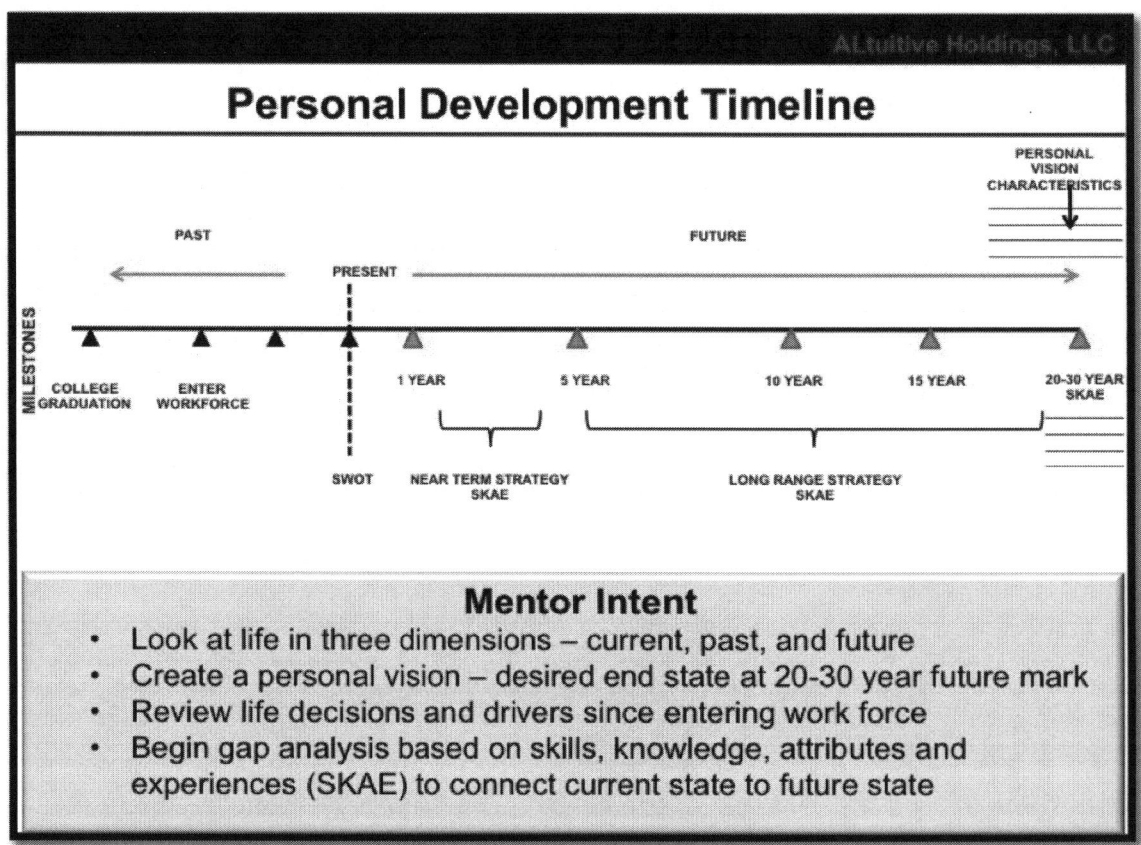

Figure 5.3 Personal Development Timeline

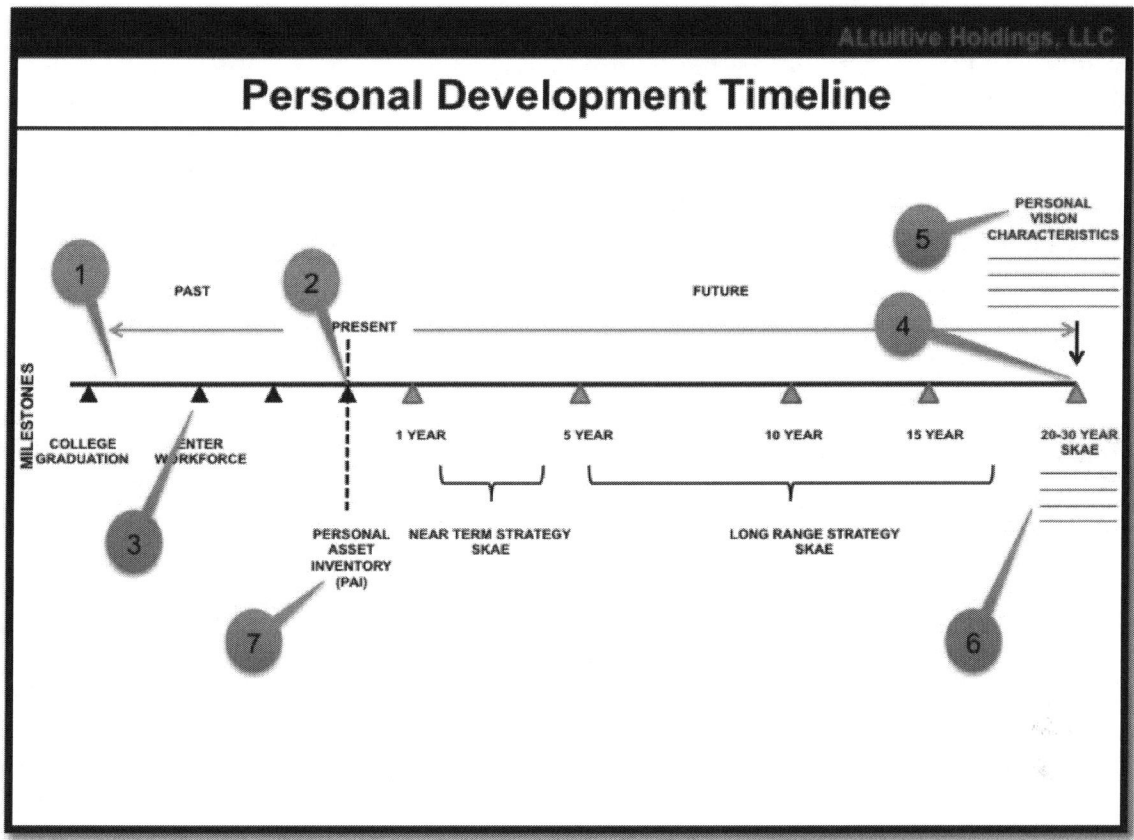

Figure 5.4 Personal Development Timeline Steps

Let's walk through the process step by step. The numbers on the chart (Figure 5.4) correspond to the text below:

1. Draw a simple horizontal line on a piece of paper.

2. On that line, add a point to represent the present. Make sure it is far enough to the right to allow listing the years and key life decisions that have taken place since entering the work force.

3. Add triangles to represent your key life decisions. During the timeline discussions, we will work together to understand why you chose a certain direction or response.

4. Visualize and characterize a successful life 25-30 years in the future. In my experience very few people take the time to declare a long-term future, much less, to build life strategic plans to achieve their goals.

5. Describe your personal vision with concrete phrases such as, "independently wealthy," "married with children and grandchildren," "homeowner," "world traveler," "own my own business," "serving on a board of directors for a non-profit," "healthy," "spiritually fulfilled," "VP of a large company," whatever your dreams are made of. Give your vision a voice so you can start the process of building paths that will take you there. As life circumstances change, you can and should revise the timeline.

6. Define to the best of your ability the four categories – Skills, Knowledge, Attributes, and Experience (SKAE)[4] – that would be required to live the life you want to live 25-30 years out. For example, if you want to be a small business owner, you need to have the basic business skills, knowledge of what it takes to own a business, the kind of personal attributes that are required to successfully start up and run a business, and some experiences that prepare you for the challenges you are likely to face. There is a smart power behind using the SKAE framework because it is a simple, useful tool to perform a career gap analysis.

7. After following the previous six steps, take the time to review your current Personal Asset Inventory (PAI) developed in the previous phase. Use the PAI to identify your current SKAE. Compare your current SKAE against the SKAE required for the future aim point. Identify the gaps. These are the areas that you will use to develop strategies to make your goals achievable.

Timeline conversations based on this tool can be very rich and empowering. Find a partner, whether mentor or significant other or peer, and talk about your input. Try to understand why previous life decisions were made, project forward to define a desired future, and leverage SKAE gap analysis to create focused goals. With proper planning and insight, you can make any desired future possible. This is personal strategic planning at the basic level. Rather than being trapped by the past, take responsibility for defining and creating a different future, one targeted at your own goals and aligned with your personal passion in life. It takes a lot of work to get to this point, but the investment in time and energy will pay significant dividends in the future.

(1) Based on your Personal Development Timeline describe your personal long-term vision. What do you want your life to look like in 25-30 years?

---

[4] Modification to the KSA (Knowledge, Skill, Ability) model commonly used in government agencies to describe job prerequisites. See www.va.gov/jobs/hiring/apply/ksa.asp

(2) What are the key skills, knowledge, attributes and experience that would be required to make this vision possible?

Skills:

Knowledge:

Attributes:

Experience:

(3) Based on your Personal Asset Inventory what are the most significant gaps between your skills, knowledge, attributes and experience today and the ones identified above as critical for your personal vision?

Skills:

Knowledge:

Attributes:

Experience:

Step 4: Developing Personal Life Strategies

At this stage you are set to begin building your personal strategy to close the gap between where you are today and where you want to be in the future. Meet with your mentor, peer or partner and discuss your SKAE gaps in the context of your Personal Asset Inventory. Allow sufficient time to review the gaps, prioritize them, and think through some alternative ways to close them. I recommend focusing on the top 2-3 areas where significant gaps exist. These "strategic thrusts" represent the high-payoff areas where personal effort can make a significant difference in closing the gaps over time. Depending on your life goals, the gaps may involve education, self-improvement, physical health, life experiences, work experiences, spiritual development, volunteer work, or any activity that addresses SKAE gaps.

(1) Document the top strategic thrusts that you intend to focus on to close your SKAE gaps:

Strategic Thrust 1:

Strategic Thrust 2:

Strategic Thrust 3:

Other:

(2) Recommended Activity: This section requires reflection, conversation and commitment. For each of the strategic thrusts you identified above, think through the specific action steps that it would take to close the SKAE gaps. Develop a basic plan of action listing specific achievable activities, milestones, and dates for completion for each of these areas. Be as specific as possible. For example, if one of your strategic thrusts is to get a Masters Degree, basic steps such as taking the GRE, applying for admission to a college, completing all prerequisites, attending classes, passing courses and graduating should all go on your timeline. The more specific you are in these action plans, the more likely you are to succeed. Most strategic thrusts will be very broad and require a number of smaller action plans. Take care to include each supporting action in your overall plan. Break down the activity into the most logical smaller steps, and track your progress against each of these steps. Adjust the action plans as life unfolds and circumstances change. Revisit your PAI and your vision, keep them current and make them "living" documents, relevant tools that you will continually use along the journey. List the action plans that you intend to develop and hold yourself accountable for below. For each of these plans I recommend you create a separate folder (physical or virtual) to document your action plans. Each folder should contain the following information: Strategic Thrust, Action Description, Incremental Steps Required For Completion, Planned Completion Dates, Dates for Review with Mentor(s), Actual Completion Date, and Comments. By using this basic structure you will leave little to chance or circumstance and increase the likelihood you will actually achieve what you set out to do.

Step 5: Executing the Discipline
(1) For Mentees: No strategy, personal or otherwise, is meaningful unless it drives deliberate, intentional action. In fact, the essence of any strategic plan is to close the gap between a current state and a desired future state by applying resources to directed actions. Everything you have done to this stage was to get you to this point. You have built the framework for crafting your life strategy. You increased your self-awareness through your Personal Asset Inventory. You built your life timeline to include describing a desired future and assessing what skills, knowledge, attributes and experience (SKAE) it will take to get you there. You did your SKAE gap analysis and identified the key areas that you intend to invest time and energy on, and you drafted achievable action plans to make incremental progress over time. Now all that remains is executing your plans and holding yourself accountable for making progress. That is the only way to make this work meaningful and move from hope to real results. To help you along the way, now more than ever before you need to be consistent with setting up meetings with your mentor. Don't get frustrated and give up if you are not making the progress you hoped for. Remember that you do not lose when you fail to meet your goals. You lose when you quit.

(2) For Mentors: During this execution phase, if you are a mentor, you can best serve as a knowledgeable, invested coach, a sounding board to offer encouragement, perspectives and support. This is the time when the workload shifts to the mentee and executing the action plans that turn hope into results. Follow-on mentor sessions should focus on tracking progress, creating disciplined accountability, and considering life changes that impact on the existing action plans. This is also the stage where it makes sense to connect the mentee to your personal network of professional contacts as needed. By this time, the mentee's commitment to positive change is evident. Leveraging your network and expending social capital on behalf of the mentee creates opportunity space and broadens the mentee's base of support. Sharing your network is one of your most important responsibilities, especially during the strategy execution phase.

If the mentee's immediate sense of urgency fades, make a call and ask how things are going. Offer to set up additional sessions. Sometimes, my mentees have been embarrassed by their own lack of progress on their journey, and in their embarrassment, let the sessions fade. This is where a gentle supportive nudge by a caring, non-judging mentor can make all the difference in the world.

A mentor's journey lasts a lifetime. As with any life skill, the more you mentor the more proficient and effective you will become at it and the more your Mentor Intelligence™ will grow. If you have made the decision to give this process a try, share that with your mentee. Let them know that you, too, are a work in progress and that you will learn as they do. You will both benefit from doing that.

I have some mentees who get frustrated with life situations yet they have not invested the time and energy on the front end of the process. They will continue to be frustrated. Until a person comes to terms with the big questions in life, the little ones are not going to make sense. This process loads the front end with that work and it provides context for everything else that happens. I constantly challenge the mentors I am training as well as my mentees to be patient, to resist the urge to jump right in and solve problems until they have built the foundation of a relationship and come to terms with the larger life questions that become visible through the ALtuitive Process.

Notes and Reflections

Notes and Reflections

Chapter Six: Tools To Empower Mentor Relationships

As you develop your skills by investing in mentor relationships, you will likely be called upon to offer your opinion about another person from time to time or to help someone make a difficult life decision. This chapter provides two tools to help you with these important tasks. As with everything else in the Field Guide and workbook, these tools can be used by anyone regardless of situation, circumstance or mentor relationship.

Tool One: A Three-Dimensional View of Human Potential
The *Talent Cube*© (Figure 6.1) is a simple visualization tool that offers a more complete view of talent. If you are ever asked to assess a person's potential, I strongly recommend using this tool as a framework for that assessment. Take the time to work through each of the Talent Cube© categories. The cube presents key dimensions of talent I believe are important to life and leadership and will always give you a more complete picture.

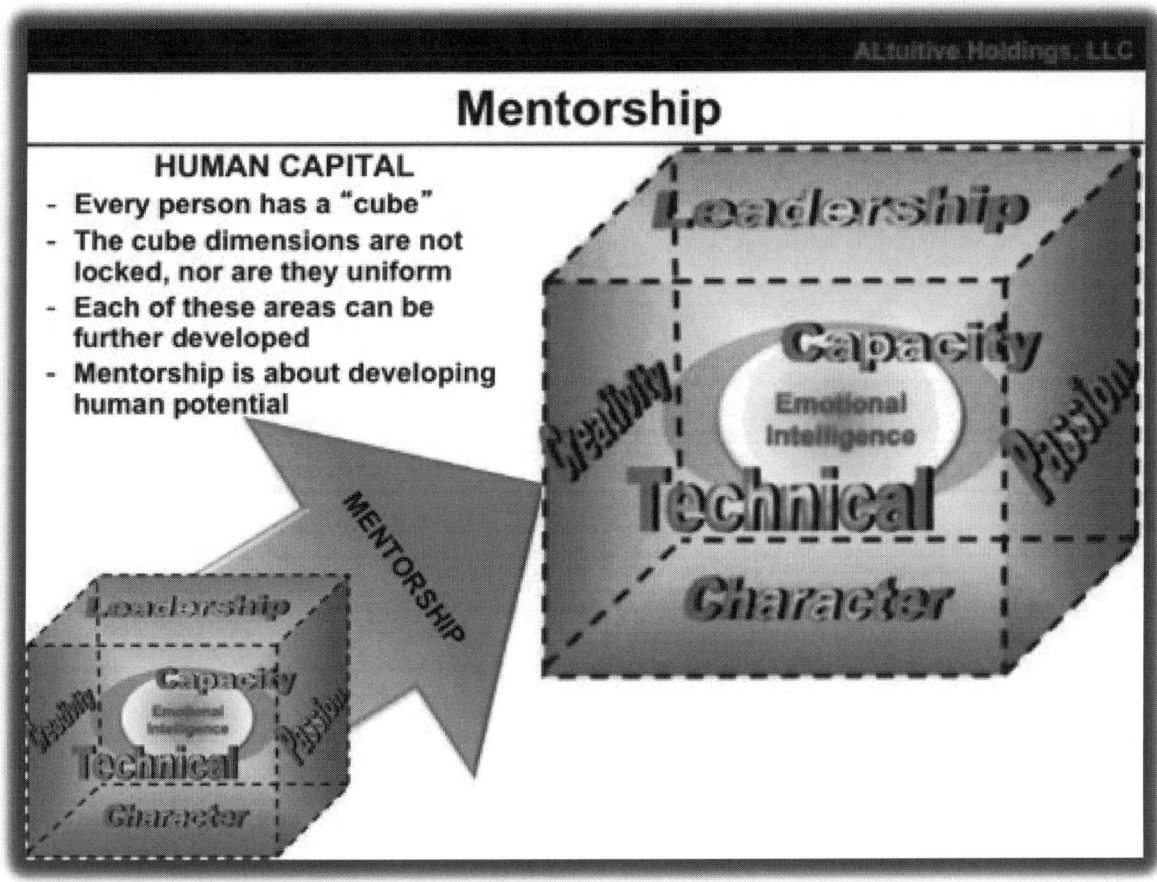

Figure 6.2 Mentorship and the Talent Cube©

Each "panel" of the cube represents a different aspect of talent important to any leader position. The panels of the cube are dashed in the illustration to indicate that growth potential exists for every person in each dimension – as a person grows in an area, that panel will expand. This is an organic view of human capital and it is a really nice way to illustrate the whole package that a person can bring to any organization or team. By considering character, leadership ability, passion, creativity, capacity and emotional intelligence in addition to technical skills, we can form a more complete view of any person's talent and set the stage for focused personal growth.

The cube is especially useful in mentoring relationships to focus energy on the most significant developmental opportunities. When combined with the PAI, Timeline and SKAE analysis, the Talent Cube can help the mentee visualize how all the pieces fit together and where the greatest opportunities for personal growth exist.

Recommended Activity: If you were to fill out an assessment on yourself using the Talent Cube© evaluating yourself in each of the 7 categories, where are your strengths and where are your greatest areas for growth? How can you use this tool to augment your self-awareness gained from the Personal Asset Inventory, Timeline and SKAE Gap Analysis?

Tool Two: Course of Action (COA) Analysis
Who does not struggle with complex life decisions? I think most of us face this challenge more often than we might care to admit. Too often, life decisions are made in the press of time, without full context or a rigorous thought process. As a result, people make the same kind of mistakes over and over, making real progress or recovery difficult. It does not have to be this way. The tools here make critical, complex decision making much easier.

Building a Course of Action Matrix

- Step 1: Define the problem to be solved
- Step 2: Define Evaluation Criteria (EC) that you will use to compare each possible option
- Step 3: Identify the alternative solutions called Courses of Action (COA)
- Step 4: Build the matrix
- Step 5: Analyze each COA against each of the Evaluation Criteria (EC); assign numerical values across the matrix
- Step 6: Compare advantages and disadvantages
- Step 7: Pick the best option

Figure 6.3 Building a COA Matrix.

This next tool is a modification of a staff process used in the US Army Military Decision Making Process (MDMP) called the Course of Action (COA) analysis.[5] Once learned, it puts you squarely in the driver's seat of life's critical decisions and becomes hugely empowering.

If you are a mentor, it's a really good idea to take the time to master this process. As you do and apply what you learn to your mentor practice, your Mentor Intelligence™ will grow and you will teach your mentees a life skill that will empower them for the rest of their lives.

Figure 6.3 shows the seven steps in the process. While these steps are not complicated, they must be followed carefully and practiced to gain proficiency. The more time and energy you apply to this process the more effective your results will be.

Step 1: Define the problem.
Many times, the problem a mentee brings to me is not the real problem, but rather, a symptom of a larger problem. If we focus on the wrong problem, we will waste precious resources and not get closer to an effective solution. It takes Mentor Intelligence™ to ask the mentee the right questions, to actively listen to the responses, and to discern whether a larger life question underlies the perceived challenge. It bears repeating that until you come to grips with the larger questions of your life (like who are you and why you are here, what are your unique gifts and where do your passions lie), the little questions (like where you work and what job you should take) won't make much sense. If you are struggling with a complex life decision, write out what you think the problem statement is and discuss it with your mentor/peer/significant other. Don't rush to failure by chasing the wrong problem!

Recommended Activity: What is the most pressing problem you are dealing with in your life today? Write it in the space below.

---

[5] US Army, *Field Manual 5-0 Army Planning and Orders Production* (Washington, D.C.: HQDA), 20 January 2005. See Chapter 3 The Military Decision Making Process for a full description.

Step 2: Define Evaluation Criteria (EC). Once the problem is defined, the next step is to identify the ***factors most important to you*** in evaluating the relative goodness of each of your choices. These factors are what we will call your Evaluation Criteria (EC). They will help you identify the advantages and disadvantages of each potential solution. Developing EC is not always a simple thing to do. If you are struggling with important life decisions, then start now – write down the factors that are most important in your life. Use loved ones and mentors as sounding boards. Once you have EC written down do your best to put them in order of priority. Chances are some will be more important than others – this is important because we will list them in priority order on the matrix.

Learning how to develop meaningful EC is an art form that takes a lot of self-awareness and reflection; it is also critical to growing your Mentor Intelligence™ It can simplify very complex, multi-dimensional problems and point you to the best solution set. It also has intrinsic value in helping you discuss alternative solutions with your loved ones.

Recommended Activity: Develop your own current list of Evaluation Criteria that you would want to use in making any complex important life decision. What are the most important considerations in your life that would generally apply across the board in framing any significant issue? (For example: job satisfaction, financial freedom, time for family) Once you build your list, discuss it with your mentor or significant other. The more candid you are with this list the better decisions you will be able to make in the larger context of your life. List your Evaluation Criteria here.

Evaluation Criteria

1.

2.

3.

4.

5.

6.

7.

8.

9.

10.

Step 3: Identify Alternative Courses of Action (COA). For most life challenges there are usually many different ways to resolve the problem. Most often, there is no apparent simple answer to the more complex challenges we face, only alternatives, each having unique advantages and disadvantages that need to be considered. The role of the mentor at this step is to help the mentee identify *all viable options* without prematurely rejecting any before the analysis has been completed. At times I have had to remind my mentees that they are trying to solve the problem by coming up with a preferred solution before doing the analysis. Sometimes it's ok to "follow your gut," but in life's bigger challenges this is usually a formula for disaster. Do the work. Do the analysis. If you invest the right time and energy up front you will make a better decision. Remember that *you* will make the ultimate decision about how to respond to the challenge. No one can do that for you. It is both, an empowering, and a sobering responsibility.

Recommended Activity: For the problem that you identified above, what are the top three COA you are considering to resolve the problem/situation? (Note: there is no magic limit to three COAs. This is just an example. In dealing with real life situations list as many reasonable COAs as you need to in order to include every major alternative.)

COA 1:

COA 2:

COA 3:

Other Possible COAs:

Step 4: Build the Matrix. You are now ready to build your first COA Matrix. You previously identified your Evaluation Criteria (EC), your problem statement, and your three alternative Courses of Action (COA). Down the left side of a single sheet of paper list the EC in priority order. Across the top list each COA. Give them short one or two word identifiers for simplicity. Use the next figure to build your own COA matrix.

Course of Action (COA) Matrix

EVALUATION CRITERIA \ COURSE OF ACTION	COA 1	COA 2	COA 3
1.			
2.			
3.			
4.			
5.			
TOTAL			

Figure 5.4 Blank COA Matrix

Step 5: Analyze each COA against each EC. After laying out the EC and COA, your next step is to fill in the values for each alternative COA. You do this by analyzing each COA against each EC by assigning numerical values in each space on the matrix based on which COA is best for that particular factor. You can pick any scale that you want, but I always give the lowest number to the best COA measured against any EC and the highest number to the worst COA. It's easy to remember that #1 is best; since lower is better, the lowest total will identify the best COA, at least as measured against your selected evaluation criteria.

We also need to discuss weighting at this stage. In most cases, EC do not have equal importance. In the previous step you arranged your EC in priority order. Now you need to reflect on the EC and make a decision about whether you want to give any EC greater weight in the analysis over the other EC. It's really a simple process – you just add a multiplier to that EC to reflect its importance. If one EC seems to be twice as important as another, give it a 2x multiplier. Hence, the best COA against that EC would have a value of 2 x 1=2, while the worst COA against that EC would have a value of 2 x 3=6. Weighting makes it quite a lot easier to separate options based on what is most important to you, but weight judiciously! If the EC are relatively close in terms of importance to you, leave the weighting alone, but if they are not, make sure that you differentiate in the analysis.

Although this kind of analysis can be done by anyone alone, I strongly advise doing it as a team – mentor and mentee, or mentor partners. The back-and-forth dialogue is useful and forces a richer analysis as perspectives and opinions are shared. Having to explain your ratings to someone else also provides a level of rigor that might otherwise not be present.

Recommended Activity: After you build your draft matrix and make a decision on weighting the EC, evaluate each of your COA against each EC and provide a tentative value in each box on the matrix. Set up a meeting with your mentor/partner and go through the matrix, explaining why you gave each rating. Think through your rationale and adjust as you see fit based on the conversation. Make sure you give the other person a chance to comment. Try not to be defensive; sometimes we fall in love with our own work and fight if someone challenges it. At this point in the process, you *want* to be challenged so invite it. If you are too defensive, you are likely to shut the other person down and they will reward you with silence. In the space below write down your observations from doing this exercise. What did you learn? Did you change anything in your matrix (COA, EC, or ratings)?

Step 6: Compare advantages and disadvantages. Now it's time to consider the results of the analysis by checking out the totals at the bottom of the matrix. Assuming that you followed the general guidelines in the previous steps, the COA with the lowest total is the best option, at least as considered against your EC. The COA with the highest total will be the worst COA against those same criteria. Many times, this first pass at the matrix helps identify other factors that should be included in the analysis. It is also very common during this first review that one or more of the EC are seen as so critical to the decision that it needs to be weighted in comparison to the other EC as previously discussed. In these cases, simply multiply the value of the EC by the desired factor. For example, if the EC is twice as important as the other factors, the scale becomes "2, 4, and 6" rather than "1, 2 and 3."

With the first review complete, it's time to assess what you learned about each COA. Write down the advantages and disadvantages of each option based on the values assigned and talk them through with your mentor partner. There is seldom a perfect or simple answer – every COA will have plusses and minuses that have to be considered. The value of the COA Analysis is that it offers a simple way to consider very complex issues by breaking them down into smaller components that are important to you. More importantly, because you took the time to build a matrix, you now have a wonderful way to share your problem with others in a way that puts everything on the table.

Recommended Activity: Given your problem statement, COA matrix and conversations with others, write down the advantages and disadvantages of each COA below.

	COA1	COA2	COA3
Advantages			
Disadvantages			

Step 7: Pick the best option. After advantages and disadvantages are reviewed, it's time to make a decision. If you have put in the work up front, this should be the easy part, even if the decision is not an easy one to make.

If you are still uncomfortable with the answer you came up with, perhaps you left out a critical EC or another possible COA. It happens. This is the point where engaging your significant others (again) can be more important than talking with your mentor. Either way, talk your concerns out, give them a voice and share them with someone important to you.

You may want to consider a hybrid COA – one that is a blend of the others, or perhaps even a completely different one that came up in the process. This is a perfectly acceptable outcome. Just don't rush to failure. Take the time to assess the revised COA against the same EC and redo the matrix.

The other value of this process beside the visualization it provides is that it better prepares you to monitor impacts and outcomes as the decision is executed. This way you can adjust the decision as facts surrounding the problem become clearer over time. New options and new possibilities emerge as the fruits of this effort, empowering you to retain ultimate control of the situation.

Recommended Activity: Now that you have completed your first COA analysis, document your decision and your rationale below.

Why did you make the decision that you did?

What are you going to watch for during the execution?

What would cause you to change to another COA? Share these notes with your mentor/mentee partner/significant other so they can support you during the execution phase.

What's In Your Life's Tool Box?
Throughout this workbook you have learned practical tools that can be used to sort through tough challenges at home or at work. All of them have been used in my mentor practice and they work. My hope is that mentors, mentees and mentor partners alike will take these tools, learn them, apply them in their own journeys, and take them to the next level! For anyone seeking more effective mentor relationships and better life decision making, these tools can reduce the complexity and frustration we all struggle with from time to time, and teach valuable life skills in the process. Learn them and you will grow your own Mentor Intelligence™.

Notes and Reflections

Notes and Reflections

Chapter Seven: Mentoring From The Heart

Here are ten reflections designed to stimulate your thinking and increase your personal Mentor Intelligence™.

1. The Power of Two^E

As I wrote The Field Guide, I reflected on the increasing isolation that seems to affect all of us in one way or the other. Isolation can grip a person's soul. Feeling alone and secluded, these people, each a special and unique creation of God, can act out in unimaginable and destructive ways. It does not have to be this way. We have a choice, each of us, to ignore the separation around us or to connect and create an alternative path of hope and promise rather than anger, pain and destruction. Our young people need a hand-up today, not a hand out. They need us to connect with them at the life level, talk to them like they are real people with good minds and capable hearts, and give them a human connection to counter the loneliness and isolation so many of them feel. This is what mentorship is all about; it's what I call "The Power of Two." I gained this enabling insight from a very special mentor who has taken my life and my thoughts about mentorship to the next level. His name is Tom Tuohy (pronounced "Two-ee"). Tom is the founder of a non-profit organization called Dreams for Kids (DFK).[6] This organization teaches at risk youth career and life skills as they build social enterprises to make the world a better place. DFK turns the world of isolation and loneliness for disadvantaged youth upside down. As they learn and grow, they move from being the problem to being the solution. This changes the world one kid at a time.

Tom's personal example of the "Power of Two" is about taking one extraordinary step to reach out to another human being without expectation or judgment to give life new meaning and purpose. It is about teaching someone to rise above circumstance, disadvantage, adversity, or disability and creating new possibility in another person's life. It is about owning a future created by deliberate personal example. It is about living a life of significance through mentorship. It is also the finest example of organizational mentorship that I know encompassing Tom, his staff, his board of directors, and his army of volunteers.

Each of us has the opportunity to live the "Power of Two" every day. Reach out to someone else today, take a chance, take the risk, make a real connection and find the meaning of significance in your own life. By combining our talents, our skills and our personal efforts, we can take the power of two to the next level and create critical mass – that is what "The Power of Two^E" represents as our efforts converge and combine to change our world for the better.

a. Recommended Activity: Make the decision today to reach out and invite at least one other person to join you in mentorship. These can be mentors, mentees or peers. Consider reaching out to a non-profit. Just make the personal decision to *do something* for someone else. Then do it. In the space below, declare your personal commitment to improve the world by making a difference in one other person's life. Who will you reach out to today and what will you commit to? When? If you put it on your calendar is it more likely to happen

---

[6] See www.dreamsforkids.org

2. Life-Changing Reverse Mentorship

This section is written especially for mentors. In my earlier mentoring years, I focused more on offering my mentees the benefit of my wisdom rather than on discerning the wisdom I might be able to gain from them. As I grew as a mentor and a leader, I began to understand I was turning my back on a valuable resource. Opening my ears (and my heart) to what I might learn from my mentees has provided me with some of my life's richest insights. Most importantly it has taught me that the most effective mentoring is about listening and reflecting more than talking. Reverse mentoring is about learning from your mentees and creating mutually supportive relationships in the process. While your mentees may not have your years of experience, they bring their own experiences, perspectives and insights that can be of great value in your life if you give them a place.

Recommended Activity: If you are a mentor, write down the top 3-5 insights you have gained from those you mentor.

How did those insights change your life?

Have you told your mentees they have made a difference to you? If not, call them up and do it now.

3. Making Time For What Is Most Important

Mentoring is a personal choice. The best leaders I have met treat mentoring as a "required-to-do" activity. They understand it is a basic leader responsibility to nurture the next generation of leaders. They make time in their routine, no matter how busy they are or how high they climb in their particular organization, to make mentoring happen.

Rather than viewing this from the perspective of your time, let's consider it from the perspective of need. Look around the organizations you belong to. How are things going? What is the mood of your team? Are employees feeling more or less secure about their jobs and their careers? When you make time to talk with the newest employees, what do they tell you about the climate of the organization? Let need define your actions rather than time. We can always find excuses or say we are already doing enough. Said enough times, it may even sound convincing, at least in our own minds. Yet when we look at it objectively, that will only sustain the status quo in our organizations. If nothing changes, nothing changes!

Make the time to mentor, make it part of your routine whatever that routine is, and know that at the end of every day, what you do here will matter far more than what happens at most required organizational meetings. At the end of the day, people grow the business, the organization, the team, the church the club, or any team you belong to, not meetings and not machines. The more we all invest in the development of our teams, the more they will deliver for us and for our organizations. The competitive advantage of any organization rests with its people – enough said!

Recommended Activity: If you are a mentor or consider yourself to be a leader, take a look at your calendar and go back at least 6 months. Over that period, how much time did you make for mentoring?

How does that align with what you have told your team?

Are you "walking your talk" with your personal example?

If you have an admin who schedules your meetings, what have told him/her about the importance of mentor sessions?

How many mentor sessions have you canceled over the past 6 months?

4. Group Mentoring - The Magic of ELSWG

Are you a senior manager in your organization or higher? Does your organization consist of several functional organizations or profit and loss centers? If so, have you given any thought to creating a cross-functional or cross-organizational mentor group?

In the Field Guide, I discuss my own journey leading to the creation of such a mentoring group called Emerging Leader Strategy Work Group (ELSWG for short). I recruited a young engineer in our company to help me find ten or so early career employees. I wanted them to be a diverse group (i.e., not all white male engineers) and asked that each candidate be "acknowledged as a leader by their peers." Unlike the elitist leader programs I discussed earlier in the Field Guide, I wanted to include the kinds of emerging leaders often excluded by circumstance or visibility in these more formal programs. At the time I was serving as strategy director for our organization. My intent was to create a small group of early career leaders with whom I could share the strategy on a more personal and engaged level. I wanted to take some positive action to close the mentor gap I observed in our organization. I also wanted to help our business thrive.

I established 1 ½ hour monthly sessions where I provided lunch for the group. We would meet for dialogue, lively conversation, and mentoring. Over time our topics grew to include leadership, diversity and inclusion, difficult conversations, dealing with adversity, tough business decisions, personal life-work balance, health, and a host of other topics usually suggested by one of the attendees. Every month attendance would vary depending on individual schedules. Since members came from the breadth and depth of the organization, we never had the exact same group present, which only added to the richness. To expand our reach to those who could not attend each session and to offer ELSWG access beyond the meetings, we created an e-room where members could post material and review anything covered by the group during the meetings. The room became the team's repository for presentations on strategy, leadership philosophies and insights, team member MBTI® profiles and dealing with different personality types, group input on work challenges and difficult situations, dealing with adversity and turning it into advantage, book reviews, and other think pieces of value to the team.

Over time, and even with varied attendance, the sessions became deeper, more candid, and more insightful as the years passed and our relationships grew. ELSWG became "mentorship glue" for the members, a place to have safe, authentic conversations about important topics, and most importantly, we created a unique network of emerging leaders with influence across the organization. We grew our Mentor Intelligence™ as a team of connected, caring colleagues.

I share this experience to inspire others to step out, to see the mentor vacuums where they exist, and to do something about it. Not only is group mentorship possible, it is also the most powerful forum for reverse mentorship that I have ever experienced. Mentorship can change a life – group mentorship can change many lives at a time including the life of the mentor.

Recommended Activity: In the organizations that you belong to, is there any opportunity for group mentorship? Regardless of opportunity, is there a need? If you are a leader in the organization, what are you willing to commit to in order to create such a group? If you are not yet a leader in your organization, are you willing to suggest the idea of a mentor group to your leadership?

5. Virtual Mentorship

While technology has unquestionably contributed to our increasing isolation, it has also provided the opportunity to conduct mentor sessions across time and space. The mobility of our society almost guarantees that we will not spend our lives in one location. Unlike our parents and their parents who frequently lived and died where they were born, today's generations are more likely to experience living in more than one location, perhaps even in different countries.

In mentorship, the advantages and the impact are the same. When distance prevents face-to-face sessions, virtually any videoconferencing technology can provide meaningful alternatives. Although none of them has the same impact as physically being there, they are good enough to use in mentor sessions. Mentorship, even if virtual, can continue over a lifetime across time and space.

Recommended Activity: If you are a mentor, attempt to use videoconferencing for one of your mentoring sessions. Learn how to use the available technology to connect with your mentees no matter where they are. If you have fallen away from one of your mentees due to relocation, use social media to catch up with them and renew your relationship. If you are a mentee or in a peer mentor relationship, ask your mentor or partner to conduct a mentor session via video-conferencing.

How did it work for you? How can you use technology to enhance your Mentor Intelligence™?

6. Lifelong Learning

This is another principal of mentorship and it's more about attitude than anything else. In my view, when inquiry stops in a person, that person is no longer capable of serving as an effective mentor. If you stop learning, how can you ask anyone else to grow?

Sustained continuous improvement and lifelong learning can increase the potential and maximize the capability of any team. If you lead by example as a mentor you can create a culture of openness to change and lifelong learning that will extend far beyond the workplace. Share your own journey, be vulnerable to learning, and this will attract people to join you in a climate of mutual respect.

Recommended Activity: Make the decision to learn something every day. Commit to it. I recommend keeping a journal to document your journey of growth and discovery. Be particularly attentive to recording lessons about life, leadership and mentorship. When things go wrong, take the time to document your lessons learned. Over time, you personal journal will become a valued and trusted partner. If you are a team leader, is there a person on your team that is challenging to work with? Has that person stopped learning about himself? Take a chance and meet offline with that person. Offer to serve as a personal coach or mentor to make the team more effective. How does working with that person impact the team? How is the individual reacting? Is he/she willing to do their part to grow? What have you gained from the experience as well?

7. Active Mutual Support
Several years ago I was exposed to the powerful concept of active mutual support.[7] At its core, active mutual support is about owning every relationship, good as well as bad, and investing time, talent and energy in the success of those you like as well as those you do not like. It is about taking the lead to repair relationships when they break. By shifting the focus of a relationship breakdown from the other person to yourself and owning the personal responsibility to invest in that person's success, you turn the world upside down. Fractured relationships can be fixed as long as one side is willing to take the first step. Even if there is no response from the other party, this act is where the moral high ground lies.

Recommended Activity: Are you currently in a relationship with a family member/ coworker/significant other that has become strained or fractured? Have you done anything to resolve the situation? If not, make the time to meet with that person for a cup of coffee or a lunch and tell that person that you value him/her, that you are sorry that your relationship has become strained and for any part that you played in creating that situation, and that you want to repair the relationship. Talk about the concept of active mutual support and what it means to you. Be vulnerable and open to whatever the other person says. In relationships, there is no competition and it's really not about winning. It's about staying in relationship no matter what. This is the essence of creating a win-win. Give it a try and write down your experience with this concept. What did you learn? What was the impact of your candor and vulnerability on the other person? How can you apply what you learned to your other relationships?

8. Advocacy
In the practice of mentoring, advocacy means leveraging your personal resources to advance the career growth of a mentee. Typically, advocacy involves making personal recommendations on behalf of the mentee when position openings occur, providing introductions to other senior leaders, sharing professional networks, writing letters of recommendation, setting up meetings with subject matter experts in fields of interest, preparing mentees for interviews, and any number of other requests that make personal resources available to the mentee. At its most basic level, advocacy is about staking your reputation on mentees by presenting them to your inner circle of professional contacts. Personal recommendations carry a lot of weight and can make the difference between selection and non-selection for competitive positions. Because of the gravity of providing personal advocacy, be selective about what you offer, when you offer it, and to whom, not only to protect your reputation with peers and supervisors, but also to protect your mentees by not diluting the value of the resource.

---

[7] More information on the concept of active mutual support can be found at www.arbinger.com

As with every other aspect of good mentoring, advocacy is an iterative process requiring deliberate action and solid follow through. Mentor Intelligence™ plays a crucial role in this process, so the more developed a mentor's skills become, the more adept and effective they become as advocates.

Recommended Activity: Make a list of your professional contacts and the areas of expertise they represent. Contact each of them and talk about your mentor practice. Ask for their support as potential resources for your mentees on an as-needed basis. As you consider referring mentees to them, set the stage by contacting your resources first to let them know to expect a call or visit from your mentee. Ask mentees to set up meetings with your contacts as you see fit. Follow up with both the contact and the mentee to see how the session went. Following this simple process sets the stage for successful advocacy and ensures accountability across the board.

9. Decision-Making Skills

Every person is eventually faced with critical life decisions that are complex, have multiple options for resolution, and involve both practical and emotional issues. Of all the recommendations in the book, none is more important for mentors and mentees than mastering some process for critical decision-making. In the previous chapter I offered the COA Matrix as one useful approach. This decision-making tool puts sanity, focus and objectivity as counter-balances to the emotional content and "gut check" that we all tend to rely on. It works. More importantly, it creates self-reliance and empowerment while growing Mentor Intelligence™ for anyone who uses it.

Recommended Activity: Consider a situation that you are personally dealing with that has multiple variables and possible outcomes. Take one hour in a location free from distractions and walk through the seven steps of the COA analysis tool presented in the previous chapter. What did you learn by using the process? What parts of the process were harder for you to work through? Consider sharing your work with a significant other. Capture your observations in the space below.

10. Abundance Thinking vs. Scarcity Thinking

This final contemplation is about creating a positive and constructive life-view as the foundation for your Mentor Intelligence™. There are two different types of people in this world: those who are able to see, and create, win-win possibilities in life for others (abundance thinking) and those who believe that the only way for one person to gain is for another person to lose (scarcity thinking). Steven Covey created this concept in his seminal work, "The Seven Habits of Highly Effective People."[8] Abundance thinking is not about unrealistic optimism nor is scarcity thinking just about unbridled pessimism. Good leadership and good teams need a healthy balance of both optimism and realism to create effective solutions. The nuance here is that leaders who embody abundance thinking are able to take the negatives in any situation and create positive outcomes for themselves and for others.

---

[8] Steven Covey, *The Seven Habits of Highly Effective People* (New York: Simon and Schuster, 1989), 219-220.

Scarcity thinkers typically create a world of winners and losers, and that is what they teach. To them, winning is more important than anything else, including relationship. In this worldview losers lose because they deserve to. It is both destructive and dangerous, especially to those who are most at-risk or disadvantaged – diversity and inclusion are certain casualties.

In any life situation, each of us has the power to create lose-lose outcomes (the typical outcome of scarcity thinking), win-lose outcomes (the actual goal of scarcity thinking), or win-win outcomes (the real goal of abundance thinking). It is always more challenging to create those win-win outcomes. It takes more effort, more humility, more compassion, more empathy and more understanding. This is what Mentor Intelligence™ is really all about. It nurtures relationships and creates future possibilities scarcity thinkers cannot envision or achieve.

Guiding a mentee to see possibility where they did not, relationship where they could not, and growth where they would not, is high art, and represents one of the highest forms of personal mentorship. Sometimes, it is as simple as asking a mentee to envision what that elusive win-win would look like – something no scarcity person would ever ask. If you can envision it you can make it happen.

It can also be a very humbling experience to watch mentees grow to become morally balanced, ethical and effective leaders, able to turn adversity into advantage for others, not just for themselves. For any leader there are few things as challenging as learning how to take what seems to be a negative situation (such as a draw down or disciplining a team member) and navigating a solution set that strengthens the team rather than weakening it, even if it comes at the expense of individual members. Abundance thinking balances pragmatism, judgment, discernment and hope to create that solution set.

Abundance thinking is also about making room in your mentality and behavior for diversity and inclusion. Scarcity thinking at its core is about judging others as "less worthy" and hence, less deserving. It is only in abundance thinking that we create a level playing field regardless of advantage or privilege. This is "mentoring from the heart."

Recommended Activity: Reflect on your life choices and commit to a mentorship practice based on abundance thinking. If you are a mentor, use your next mentor session to expose your mentees to the concept of abundance thinking. Take a relationship problem the mentee is struggling with and help him/her visualize the characteristics of a "win-win" situation. What would it look like for both parties? What would it take to create that situation? How can they repair the fracture without creating a losing situation for anyone in the process? If you are a mentee or a partner in a peer mentorship situation, have the courage to be open to the concept of abundance thinking and use it to grow your own Mentor Intelligence™. Use the space below to record your reflections and experiences with abundance thinking.

Notes and Reflections

Notes and Reflections

Chapter Eight: Leading For Life

Leadership is the glue that holds the threads of Mentor Intelligence™ together. Leadership and mentorship are intertwined. Good leaders are good mentors. Leadership can't be taught or learned from a checklist. It has to be developed in a way that honors the creation each of us represents with our diverse experiences, personalities, skills and talents.

There are many books available about the character traits and styles of good leadership for anyone who wants to learn more about the topic. They are useful as a general framework for developing a style of leadership that works best for you. Over time I began to reflect on the fact that effective leadership style is extremely personal – what works authentically for one person may not work for another.

So just as the ALtuitive approach to mentorship is question-based rather than answer-based, I offer a question-based leadership ecosystem based on eight core questions every leader should ask before making any decision affecting the life of another person. These are questions we can all embrace and make relevant to our lives. You can use them as a guide in navigating your own leadership situations. With each passing decision, you will be increasing your Mentor Intelligence™. Copy the chart included in the Field Guide and put it up on the wall in your office as a reminder anytime you have to make a significant leader decision. Answer the questions candidly and reflect on the reasons for your answers in each situation. It might change how you decide and what you decide.

A Leadership Ecosystem: Eight Questions For Reflection and Action

Question 1: When you make a leadership decision, from what direction are you leading?
Each of us has experienced "leaders" who were more concerned about their bosses than their teams. It is more rare, but occasionally I have seen leaders who were just the opposite – they were so overly concerned about their teams that they were reckless with their leadership. Seldom mentioned is the impact of lateral considerations, how what you do on your team impacts surrounding teams. Taken to an extreme, that can lead to groupthink, or on the other end, to unhealthy competition. As you consider any leader situation, take the time to consider your motivations. Why are you doing what you are doing? Who will benefit? What is the impact in all three directions?

In the military, we used to have this saying about running to the sound of the gunfire. It is an analogy for leading from the front, having the courage to expose yourself to the same danger and risk that your team faces. When problems hit your team, how do you respond? Do you jump into the fray or sit back and send in your teammates? In times of challenge do you engage yourself and become part of the solution or turn the problem (and the risk) over to others? Do you have the courage to include your team in the decision? Good leadership is conscious leadership, leadership that knows motive and assesses impacts in every direction. Before you decide, reflect on this. From what direction are you leading, and why?

Question 2: How do you inform your leadership decisions?
As senior leaders move up in their organization's ranks, it seems at times that they value <u>what they know</u> far more than <u>what they do not know</u>. There are blind spots in every situation. Sometimes administrative staff subjectively block information from a leader in an attempt to prioritize time on the calendar – the higher the staff it seems the greater the filter. This is not a criticism against administrative assistants or staffs – they do what their leaders expect them to do. The very best leaders I know understand that and are very careful to ensure their "gatekeepers" (staff) know they value time for mentoring. They are also sensitive to how easy it is to create the wrong impression by saying one thing and doing another.

Before making any critical decision a thoughtful leader will take a step back, assess what is known and how it is known, think about how reliable the information is, identify where the gaps are and why they exist, and determine actions that can be taken to close them. It is wise to include others in the information-gathering process and filter fact from fiction.

Two practical examples of this kind of leadership action are skip-echelon meetings and unannounced visits to unexpected locations within the organization. It is amazing what leaders can discover about themselves and about their organizations by breaking routine and being open to what they do not know. In every case, these actions will result in better, more informed decisions. Where are your blind spots and what are you doing to shine the light on them before you make a decision?

Question 3: What do you reflect to your team?
This question is fascinating and important. I have often shared with my mentees that the only part of your body that you cannot see without a mirror is your face. Yet to the rest of the world, your face (closely coupled to the tone of your voice) is the mirror to your soul. It speaks volumes about what you really feel. You may intend to send out an innocuous message to someone on your team and you get a completely unintended negative or defensive reaction. The disconnection is not always in our word choices (although that's important too), it's often in the facial expressions that we do not see, and in our tone of voice. From the time we are babies, we learn how to read and respond to them. They convey your real intent. They can convey acceptance or rejection and they have the power to lift up or to destroy.

When you look at your team members, especially during challenging times, what do they see? Do they see a critic who focuses more on faults and limitations or do they see a caring leader who focuses more on qualities and potential? Every leader needs to develop his or her team, and that means acknowledging faults, problems and shortfalls. But that can be done in a destructive way or in a constructive way, and the choice will be evident in your facial expressions and tone of voice.

There is also a very important implication to diversity and inclusion here. We all know leaders who are not inclusive, who only want to be around those most like them. When they get someone "different" on the team, their facial expressions will say a lot about their behavior and their willingness to be open to the differences or not, regardless of what they say.

This leads to the final point – "walking the talk." These are the three most important words in any leader's life. If you speak about respect, diversity and inclusion, and openness as a leader, but your actions are not aligned with those words, you will not be credible to anyone. Walk the talk, be visible, and let your actions, words, and tone speak to your real character. How do you hold yourself accountable to your team for this critical aspect of leadership? How do you know? What are you willing to do to find out?

Question 4: How do you wield your power as a leader?
At its most basic level, leadership is about exerting power over another person's life. That power can be intoxicating, especially for the emerging leader experiencing it for the first time. I have observed leaders who wielded that power almost as if it were a divine right. This is not about self-confidence – all effective leaders must be self-confident - this is about arrogance and egocentric leadership. If such self-centered "leaders" succeed, it will almost always come on the backs and shoulders of their people. An interesting question – if you assess the percent of your leaders that are self-serving, what would that percent be for your organization? I know there is a tipping point – but I confess that I do not know where that is. For now, look at it as an important observation and come up with your own answer for your own organization.

There is another perspective. Many leaders that I have known, and served with, accept that any leadership position is a gift and exercise power with deep personal humility. Do your own research and come up with your own role models. They really are easy to find. Humility can lead to an open heart, an open mind and an open soul. There is a *quiet power* that comes from shifting the focus of your leadership from yourself to your team. It makes others want to work for you because they believe in you and trust you to do the right thing for them and the team rather than doing what increases your influence. A humble leader never loses sight of the responsibility to nurture, develop and grow the team. Interestingly, these are the leaders who are never forgotten, even if they are not written about.

Leader results versus intent is another important consideration. It is never enough as a leader to have good intent. Good intent on any leader's part is a given. Leadership is about generating *good results* based on that good intent. How many times have you heard someone say, "I did not intend for that to happen," or "that's not what I meant, you did not hear me correctly!" The leader is responsible for whatever happens, intended or not. Good leaders are not satisfied until the desired good effect is achieved. When leaders focus as much on result as on intent, goodness always results.

This applies to critical leader communications as much as it does to actions. If you have a message that you want to deliver to a person or a team, sending the message is just step one, yet that is often where things stop. Monitoring how that person or your team responds is step two, and adjusting the *message*, the *medium* or the *tone* is step three. Leader follow-through is not micromanaging; it is a basic leader responsibility. The job is not over until the desired results are achieved. The burden is on the sender, not the receiver, the leader not the led. How do you wield your own leadership power? What would your team say? What would your bosses say? How can you make sure that your results always match your intent?

Question 5: To whom do you point for your and your team's successes? What about for failures?

One of the greatest leadership quotes came from President Harry Truman when he said, "It's amazing what you can accomplish if you do not care who gets the credit."[9] Yet in today's highly charged, competitive workplace, credit seems to matter more each day. The important leader question is how you manage, share, and balance it. Teams, not individuals, win. The most successful leaders I have known were masters at the art of giving credit to their teams. There were two discernable results: (1) those teams always did better than the other teams, and (2) the leaders of those teams were highly respected, admired and greatly valued by their subordinates.

Ambition has both a good side and a bad side. On the good side, it can fuel the drive to accomplish positive things. On the negative side, it can create credit hogs – destructively competitive teams and leaders who always want to be in the spotlight with their latest success and who go out of their way to make others look bad. That is the kind of leader no one wants to work for.

What kind of leader are you? What is your brand? Are you the leader who never misses the chance to promote the team? Or are you seen as a person who craves the credit at the expense of others?

Question 6: What do you leave in the wake of your decisions?

Imagine that you are floating on a boat in a lake. Behind you are all the people that you have encountered since you got up this morning – your family members, the people in their cars on the highway, the people you walked past in the parking lot at work, the administrative staff at the front desk who greeted you, the colleagues you passed in the hall at work, the people on your team - each of them in their own boats. Now ask yourself this question: What kind of ripples did you create in their lives today with your passing? Did you create ripples that hurt or upset them or did you help them on their own journeys?

I love this visualization because I think it reflects what really happens every day in each of our lives. We pass others and they pass us, and in the passing, we create opportunities to make a positive or a negative difference. Simple acts of kindness and compassion, doing something nice for another person and calling them by their name, the smallest of acts can create ripples that lift another person up. The power of actions like this for both the leader and the led can be understood more fully by reading *Resonant Leadership* by Richard E. Boyatzis and Annie McKee.[10]

Know that as a leader, you have the power to create positive and negative ripples in the lives of your team members every day. Without expecting anything in return, you can empower them to grow beyond even what they see in themselves. Instead of focusing on their shortfalls and inadequacies, you can choose to focus on their gifts and their strengths. You can provide opportunity beyond their wildest dreams and make their dreams possible. At the end of the day, this will be your true legacy. It will not be in what you accomplished, but in what you left behind in the lives of those you led.

---

[9] Harry S. Truman quotes (American 33rd President of the United States, 1884-1972)
[10] Richard Boyatzis and Annie McKee, *Resonant Leadership* (Boston: Harvard Business School Press, 2005)

What are the ripples you are creating? Do you even take the time to see them for what they are? What is the collateral damage of your leadership decisions? How do you motivate and inspire while creating an environment of personal and team accountability?

Question 7: What is the source of your personal funding?
While there is considerable confusion about who first said "There are no atheists in foxholes,"[11] there is no doubt about its meaning. This is not about religion; it is about believing in a higher life source that frames the answers to the larger questions in your own life. Leadership is a battlefield, complex and full of risk to both the leader and the led. I believe that self-centered leadership is toxic, not only to the team but also to the leader. I also believe there is a connection between humility and believing in a higher life source. Leaders who believe they have all the answers to life's challenges within themselves are bound to eventually stumble on a situation that defies their best efforts. As they fall they take their teams with them. Whatever your source of spiritual funding, acknowledging it as a centerpiece in your life will help you become a better, more caring, and ultimately, more effective leader.

What do you really believe in? When you reflect on your own failures and shortcomings, who do you turn to for discernment and sound judgment?

Question 8: When you are gone, what will be left behind, and will it really matter?
This final leader question is about perspective. There are a lot of very successful people in this world who are terribly unhappy. For many of these leaders, the rise to the top came at the expense of everything else important in their lives. This is the true cost of self-importance. If that is what you seek, that is what you will end your life with, nothing but yourself.

When you are gone, who will care? After all your promotions and raises and successes and accomplishments fade, what will be left? How will it define your life on this earth? Will it matter or will it evaporate the minute you pass? If you invest in others, there is no greater return for any life investment. To put this in perspective, my Army Chaplain friend Tim Bedsole once said that on their deathbeds, he never saw any person ask for a promotion, title, position or pay raise. Without exception, he said that every person asked for three things – relationship with self, relationship with their God (defined any way you like), and relationship with their family and friends. At the end of the day, that is the true definition of a life of significance.

---

[11] "There are no atheists in foxholes" in *Wikipedia: The Free Encyclopedia*; (Wikipedia Foundation Inc., updated 4 April 2013, 5:52 UTC

Notes and Reflections

Chapter Nine: Taking Flight

I hope this workbook has given you inspiration and some useful tools to grow as person, as a leader, and as a better mentor/mentee. What are you going to do with the knowledge? Although these exercises guide you through some disciplined frameworks, they leave lots of opportunity for you to customize your own brand of Mentor Intelligence™. You can be as creative as you want to be with it. Mentor Intelligence™ can improve the world, one life at a time, starting with you! Imagine a world where Mentor Intelligence™ is as important as the other forms of intelligence that we use to identify ourselves as mature adults; a world where we each create a vibrant legacy of deep, lasting relationships that span generations!

I challenge you to put Mentor Intelligence™ to use in your home, your place of work, and your social organizations. Actively seek others who might benefit from your own journey to gain Mentor Intelligence™ and take that first step toward creating more meaningful and valuable relationships, either as a mentor, a mentee, or simply a mentor partner. Link arms and form a community of interest wherever you are in your own life. Put these tools to use, develop your own, and add to the body of knowledge surrounding this important topic. Go back through the workbook and re-read your notes. Reflect on the changes taking place as you put these lessons to practical use in your life. That's what growing Mentor Intelligence™ is all about! The rewards will be yours for the taking.

As always, I enjoy sharing perspectives on leadership, mentorship, diversity/inclusion, building personal life strategies, or any other topics presented in the Field Guide or in this companion workbook. If you have any suggestions or recommendations for my work, please connect. Feel free to send me a request on LinkedIn if you want to share my network, or drop me a line at altuitiveholdings@gmail.com. I look forward to hearing from you, and thanks again for your interest in growing Mentor Intelligence™.

Notes and Reflections

Notes and Reflections

About the Author

COL (RET) Alan Landry is an experienced strategist and leader in both government and industry with a unique passion for mentorship developed over nearly four decades. He leverages his insights in leadership and mentorship in a fresh, novel approach that can help any person be more effective in his or her own life as well as in serving others as a mentor. Alan has been married for the past 40 years to Paula Williams. They are the very proud parents of four children and ten grandchildren. Alan and Paula are currently enjoying life in Alpharetta, Georgia, where Alan manages his consulting company, ALtuitive Holdings, LLC. Alan is also the author of *Growing Mentor Intelligence™: A Field Guide To Mentoring,* published in 2014.

Made in the USA
Middletown, DE
09 November 2023